ONE MAN, ONE VOTE

ONE MAN, ONE VOTE

WMCA AND
THE STRUGGLE FOR EQUAL REPRESENTATION

Calvin B. T. Lee
WITH THE ASSISTANCE OF ALAN KANZER

CHARLES SCRIBNER'S SONS
NEW YORK

Printed in the United States of America
Library of Congress Catalog Card Number 67-19989

KFN
5714
.L4

COVER DESIGN BY MIKE MC IVER

ACKNOWLEDGMENTS

Grateful acknowledgment is made to the following periodicals, publishers and
authors for granting permission to quote from their copyright works:

Adirondack Publishing Company, Inc.: Material from the Adirondack *Daily
Enterprise.*

Capital Newspapers: Material from the Albany *Times Union.*

Cornell Law Quarterly: John M. Harlan, "What Part Does Oral Argument Play
in the Conduct of an Appeal?" (vol. 41, 1955). © Copyright 1955 by Cornell
University.

Dow Jones & Company, Inc.: Material from the *Wall Street Journal.*

Michigan Law Review: Dean Robert McKay, "Political Thickets and Crazy
Quilts: Reapportionment and Equal Protection" (vol. 61, February, 1963) and
"Courts, Congress and Reapportionment" (vol. 63, December, 1964).

New York *Daily News.*

New York *Post.* © 1965 by the New York Post Corporation.

New York *Times.* © 1962/3/4/5 by the New York Times Company.

West Publishing Company: Tom C. Clark, "The Supreme Court Conference,"
Federal Rules Decisions (1956).

World Journal Tribune: Material from the New York *Herald Tribune* and the
New York *World Telegram and Sun.*

54643

TO MY STUDENTS

Preface

One Man, One Vote developed out of a senior seminar on American political problems which I taught at Columbia College. For two years, one semester of the seminar was devoted to reapportionment and the courts, a subject which forced students to look at constitutional problems in the context of the American political scene. This weekly confrontation of issues with inquiring and alert undergraduates was a most gratifying experience; I am indebted to all my students for inspiring me to write this study.

This book would not have been possible without the full cooperation of the litigants. Through Peter Straus, president of radio station WMCA, and his attorney, Leonard Sand, I was given access to all of their official and unofficial papers—briefs, transcripts, newspaper clippings, letters, memos, notes and files—from which I have quoted freely in the text. Their associates, Franz Allina and Michael N. Rosen, facilitated my task enormously. Mr. Sand had begun a book of his own about this litigation, but generously turned his material over to me.

I am also indebted to Mathias Spiegel, former executive assistant to the Attorney General of the State of New York, for his assistance. Dean Robert McKay of New York University Law School was a source of information as well as inspiration in my work on reapportionment. Professor Harold W. Chase's careful reading of the manuscript produced many valuable suggestions. William Weissman, my research assistant when I first looked into the subject of reapportionment, did not work specifically on this text, but his thorough preliminary research and his continued interest helped to make it a reality.

I would also like to acknowledge the assistance of Alan Kanzer, one of my most brilliant students. Although he was a recent college graduate at the time he assisted me with my research on this book, his work was always so professional and scholarly that I considered him a colleague. Finally, I must acknowledge the contribution of my secretary, Margot Maloof Kanzer, whose enthusiastic assistance and wit made even the duller moments of our research seem more worthwhile. But then she has already been rewarded; she married my research assistant.

CALVIN B. T. LEE

American Council on Education
Washington, D.C.

Contents

Preface   *ix*

Introduction   *1*

1. WMCA Decides to Litigate   *3*

The litigant—a "rock 'n roll" radio station . . . Three methods of bringing about reapportionment . . . Political questions doctrine—a stumbling block . . . Judicial restraint vs. judicial activism . . . Hopeful signs for the litigant . . . Complaint filed in Federal District Court, May 1, 1961.

2. A Case Is Begun   *12*

Hearing on request for calling a Statutory Court, June 7, 1961 . . . Designation of three-judge panel . . . Oral argument, November 15, 1961 . . . "A licking in Court"—Decision of Federal Statutory Court, January 11, 1962.

3. *Baker* v. *Carr:* A Judicial Landmark   *30*

Decision of the Supreme Court, March 26, 1962 . . . Profiles and opinions of Justices William J. Brennan, William O. Douglas, Tom C. Clark, Potter Stewart, Felix Frankfurter and John Marshall Harlan . . . Standards of fair apportionment . . . Reaction to Baker v. Carr.

4. The Politics of Apportionment   *42*

Appeal to the Supreme Court, February 5, 1962 . . . Release of a suppressed report on reapportionment, May 10, 1962 . . . Governor Rockefeller's statement on reapportionment . . . Decision of the Supreme

Court: WMCA case remanded, June 11, 1962 . . . Rankin telegram to Governor Rockefeller . . . Press and political reaction to Rockefeller statement.

5. A Trial on the Merits   *49*

Hearing before Federal Court, August 1, 1962 . . . Transcript of hearings . . . Another setback: Decision of Federal Court, August 16, 1962.

6. Before the High Court   *57*

Appeal to the Supreme Court, August 29, 1962 . . . Gray v. Sanders, March 18, 1963 . . . Arguments of the litigants, amicus curiae, and the United States Solicitor General . . . Change in judicial personnel: Profiles of Justices Byron R. White and Arthur J. Goldberg.

7. How the Supreme Court Decides   *75*

Predicting the vote of the Court . . . Conference sessions of the justices of the Supreme Court as described by Justice Clark . . . Role of the oral argument as described by Justice Harlan . . . Oral argument, November 12 and 13, 1963.

8. One Man, One Vote   *93*

Wesberry v. Sanders, February 17, 1964 . . . Profile and majority opinion of Justice Hugo L. Black . . . Decision of the Supreme Court in the Reapportionment Cases, June 15, 1964 . . . Profile and majority opinion of Chief Justice Earl Warren . . . Dissents of Justices Potter Stewart, Tom C. Clark and John Harlan.

9. Congress vs. the Court   *103*

Reaction to the Reapportionment Cases . . . Proposals in Congress to curb the Court . . . Gallup Poll on public reaction to the Supreme Court decision . . . Passage in the House of Tuck Bill to strip federal courts of jurisdiction over state districting, August 19, 1964 . . . Defeat of Senator Dirksen's cloture motion, September 8, 1964 . . . the liberals' "baby" filibuster.

10. Back to the District Court   *118*

Decision of plaintiffs to press for immediate apportionment . . . Appointment of Citizens' Committee on Reapportionment by Governor Rockefeller, July 11, 1964 . . . Hearing on Implementation Decree, July 15, 1964 . . . Sand seeks subpoena to inspect documents of Joint Legislative Committee on Reapportionment . . . "Guard Watches Guard Guarding Capitol" . . . Decision of the Federal District Court, July 27, 1964.

11. New York Reapportions Its Legislature   *133*

Legislative stalemate . . . Governor Rockefeller vs. State Democratic Chairman McKeon . . . Johnson landslide gives Democrats control of both houses for the first time since 1935 . . . Report of Citizens' Committee on Reapportionment, November 30, 1964 . . . Governor calls special session of Republican-controlled "lame-duck" legislature, December 1, 1964.

12. New York Apportionment Acts and the Courts: Part I   *146*

WMCA challenges new apportionment, January 4, 1965 . . . Hearings before the District Court, January 21, 1965 . . . Gerrymander evidence excluded . . . Apportionment Plan A held valid.

13. New York Apportionment Acts and the Courts: Part II   *153*

Apportionment Plans A, B, C and D held in violation of the state constitution by New York State Supreme Court . . . New start on reapportionment . . . Reaction of politicians . . . Appointment of former governor, Thomas E. Dewey, as counsel for New York State . . . Democratic opportunity . . . New York's highest court upholds decision declaring apportionment invalid.

14. New York Apportionment Acts and the Courts: Part III   *159*

Federal District Court Hearing, May 10, 1965 . . . Democrats attempt to avoid court ruling by passing two bills . . . Federal District Court orders election under Plan A, May 25, 1965 . . . Governor Rockefeller vetoes Democratic bills, May 27, 1965 . . . Per curiam decision of the Supreme Court, June 1, 1965.

15. The Last Word *168*

A step towards reapportionment . . . A new court challenge . . . State's highest court bars election the Federal Court had ordered, July 9, 1965 . . . Decision of Federal District Court, July 13, 1965 . . . Memorandum opinion of Supreme Court Justice Harlan, July 17, 1965 . . . The last word.

Conclusion *177*

Source Notes *179*

ONE MAN, ONE VOTE

Introduction

The Reapportionment Cases, decided by the Supreme Court in June of 1964, transformed into a constitutional mandate the principle of equal representation. Although "one man, one vote" is a compelling slogan—indeed, it sounds almost like an inevitable corollary of "all men are created equal"—a thorough understanding of this phrase requires an analysis of the development of a constitutional law doctrine, the political forces and pressures at work in American politics, the battle between city and rural areas, the emergence of suburbia, and the importance of history in the study of the American Constitution.

This book is a depth study of *WMCA* v. *Lomenzo,* one of the six Reapportionment Cases. The special value of a case study is that it adds the dimension of time to an analysis of an event, in this instance, the decision of the Supreme Court. Following the progress of a case enables the reader to analyze how the Supreme Court approaches a problem, how lawyers prepare and argue their cases, how decisions are made, and how these decisions are implemented, modified, or frustrated.

The *WMCA* case was chosen for several reasons. First, it involves one of the largest and most complex states—New York. Second, it demonstrates effectively the interaction of law and politics, of courts and legislatures. Finally, it presents the unusual feature of a litigant— a radio station—influencing action by an aggressive publicity campaign, as well as by skillful courtroom advocacy.

But *One Man, One Vote* is more than the study of a single case. It is also a study of the American democratic process at work. As such it adds to our understanding of the powers shared and wielded by the executive, legislative and judicial branches of the government;

it examines the strengths and weaknesses of federalism and questions the meaning of representative government; it reveals the influence of the communications media in the shaping of American political thought; and it ultimately suggests that it is the dynamic interaction between law and politics which makes the democratic process viable.

1

WMCA Decides to Litigate

When a "rock 'n roll" radio station carries on a crusade for reapportionment, it sounds like a publicity stunt. But when that rock and roll station is WMCA, one cannot be certain.

Located in New York City, WMCA is unique among major radio stations in that it combines popular music played by disc jockeys known as the "Good Guys" with generous doses of news and public service. WMCA was among the first radio stations to broadcast editorials and was the first to endorse a presidential candidate (John F. Kennedy). Among its other notable activities, the station has served the community by endeavors as varied as broadcasting voter information, organizing a housing complaint bureau ("Call for Action," which played an influential role in leading New York City to overhaul and reform its method of handling violators), offering a reward for information leading to the apprehension of a lynch suspect, and raising money and sending food and clothing to tenant farmers in Shelby County, Tennessee, who were evicted after they had attempted to vote.

The moving force behind WMCA is the Straus family. Nathan Straus, who instituted the station's public service commitment, served as a state senator from a district on the west side of Manhattan and had long been concerned about the unfair treatment the state accorded its city dwellers. His son and the current president of the radio station, R. Peter Straus, was a delegate to the Democratic National Conventions of 1960 and 1964. In 1960 he supported John F. Kennedy for president and in 1964 he was chairman of the State Democratic Campaign Committee. He has frequently been mentioned as a possible candidate for local or national office.

Aware that New York's most pressing problems—housing, transportation and education—were being inadequately handled by the rural-dominated state legislature, Straus was intrigued when, in January, 1961, he received a letter from Max Gross urging that WMCA resort to court action to overturn the New York apportionment.

Gross, a former New York City councilman, had long been associated with numerous reforms and welfare measures. His interest in apportionment stemmed from his realization that projects for which he strived were often frustrated by the rural-dominated New York Legislature. Failing in his efforts to get the state to reapportion itself voluntarily, Gross sought to persuade leading citizens to attempt to force reapportionment through court actions.

Upon receiving Gross' letter, Straus contacted his brother-in-law, Leonard Sand, attorney for WMCA and asked him to examine the feasibility of a law suit.

Slight of build, mild-mannered and shy; a man who speaks in a light, respectful voice without any flamboyant gestures, Sand is not the typical picture of a courtroom lawyer. He is, nevertheless, an able advocate and well-trained for the task which Straus had given him. A graduate of Harvard Law School where he was note editor of the *Harvard Law Review,* Sand later held the public posts of assistant district attorney in the Southern District of New York and assistant to the Solicitor General of the United States.

Sand immediately began to study the subject of legislative representation in New York State. He found a well-documented booklet on the subject by David I. Wells, assistant director of the political department of the International Ladies' Garment Workers' Union, particularly helpful. Wells was to become of valuable assistance not only in supplying statistics showing the need for reapportionment in New York, but also in his astute observations of the political scene. Sand found that primarily there were three ways of bringing about reapportionment: 1) have the state legislature reapportion itself by bringing a constitutional amendment for ratification to the voters; 2) amend the state constitution by convention; 3) have the existing apportionment invalidated by a court ruling.

The first possibility had been patiently but unsuccessfully tried by Max Gross and others for years. Legislators do not voluntarily vote themselves out of office. Furthermore, the distribution of the number of seats among the counties was not decided by the legislature but was governed by mathematical formulas written into the Constitution of the State of New York. Under a complex system for the Senate, the heavily-populated counties became more severely under-represented as their population increased. Similarly the constitutional provision limiting the size of the Assembly to 150 members and requiring that each county must have at least one seat, caused under-representation of heavily populated counties. This apportionment system which favored rural areas was referred to by the late Governor Al Smith, as being "constitutionally Republican."

An attempt to bring about change by constitutional convention failed in 1957. Although the state constitution allows the voters to decide every twenty years whether a convention should be held to consider constitutional changes, half of the voters in 1957 did not even vote on the question. Of those who did, 48% favored a convention and 52% did not; 1977 would be the next opportunity to again bring up the issue.

Thus Sand was left with only the alternative of going to the courts. He thoroughly researched past action of the courts in the area of apportionment. As Sand noted in a memorandum to Straus, "the law with respect to whether relief against discriminatory legislative apportionment can be obtained in a suit in the federal courts is in a great state of flux."

The major barrier which WMCA had to surmount was a 1946 case, *Colegrove* v. *Green,* wherein the Supreme Court held, in a 4-3 decision,* that questions of legislative apportionment were "of a peculiarly political nature and therefore not meet for judicial determination." In other words, the Court held that a federal court could not decide such questions. Justice Felix Frankfurter, who delivered the principal opinion of the Court, rejected the claim of three qualified voters in Illinois who asserted that, because of population shifts, the congressional districts in which they lived contained far more people than other districts did, and that consequently their proportionate representation was reduced in violation of Article I and the Fourteenth Amendment of the United States Constitution.

* Justices Jackson and Stone did not participate in the decision.

Frankfurter's reasons were, essentially, three: lack of justiciability; inefficiency of judicial remedies for malapportionment; and fear of usurpation of legislative responsibility.

A case is non-justiciable if it presents a "political question"; that is, a question which is not primarily legal but rather basically a matter of public policy and thus more appropriately the concern of the popularly elected divisions of the government, the executive and legislative. Throughout its history the Supreme Court has voluntarily refrained from exercising its jurisdiction (the power to hear cases) when it has decided that the cases involve matters of public policy. Thus the Court has refused to decide which faction should control the Rhode Island State Legislature when veritable civil war broke loose in the state; to determine whether a state has ratified an amendment to the United States Constitution; or to consider whether the United States is at war. In all of these cases the Court has called the matters non-justiciable and has stated that they should be determined by the "political" branches of the government.

According to Justice Frankfurter the apportionment controversy was non-justiciable because the litigants did not complain of "a private wrong, but a wrong suffered by Illinois as a polity." They were not being deprived of a right to vote. To speak of debasement of their vote was meaningless, for it assumed precisely what must be proved: that the voters had a constitutional right to have their vote carry as much political weight as anyone else's. Frankfurter pointed out that an apportionment based solely on population was only one possible method. Other equally valid methods might take into consideration such varied factors as geography, political divisions, and economic interests. To decide which of these systems should be used in apportioning was to enter into the "political thicket."

Frankfurter's second major argument was that there can be no effective judicial remedy for malapportionment. "No court can affirmatively re-map the Illinois districts so as to bring them more in conformity with the standards of fairness for a representative system." Thus to invalidate an apportionment could leave the state's election process in chaos. If the state did not voluntarily reapportion itself after its apportionment system was stricken down, congressional candidates might have to run at-large in a state-wide election. Moreover, the justice warned, there was serious question whether Congress would be willing to recognize the qualifications of representatives elected in such a manner. Thus the effect of a court decision overturning an apportionment might be to disfranchise all the people of the state.

Frankfurter's third major thesis was that apportionment was a legislative responsibility. "It is hostile to a democratic system to involve the judiciary in the politics of the people," he argued. "The remedy for unfairness in districting is to secure state legislatures that will apportion properly, or to invoke the ample powers of Congress."

This third argument reflects the basic tenet of Justice Frankfurter's constitutional theories: Courts should exercise self-restraint. Frankfurter's judicial heroes were Oliver Wendell Holmes, Louis D. Brandeis and Benjamin Cardozo—justices dedicated to the belief that the idea of democracy represents a commitment to the policy of allowing the people to govern themselves. The legislatures are elected by the people, responsible to them, and therefore most representative of the people's wishes. In marked contrast, the courts represent the aristocratic element of the government. Federal judges are appointed, not elected. Moreover, they hold their office for life; they can only be removed by impeachment for serious offenses. Thus, if democracy is to be given an opportunity to flourish, the courts should only interfere with legislative action when there are flagrant violations of the Constitution. Acts of legislatures carry with them a heavy presumption of constitutionality. Legislators, bound only by the requirement that their acts be reasonable, should be free to experiment and to develop new methods of dealing with social problems.

In 1960, after more than a decade of developing a new judicial philosophy to protect personal freedoms, the Court was faced with a dilemma: Its expanded activity in the area of civil rights came into conflict with its policy of refusing to entertain challenges to apportionments. In *Gomillion* v. *Lightfoot* the Court was confronted with a situation in which Negro citizens of Alabama charged that the state legislature, in order to prevent Negroes from voting in city elections, had altered the shape of Tuskegee from a square to an irregular twenty-eight-sided figure in such a manner as to eliminate from the city all but four or five of its 400 Negro voters without eliminating any white voters. The outcome of this conflict was that the Court held racial gerrymanders were unconstitutional but tried to distinguish the case on facts and principle from *Colegrove* v. *Green.*

Justice Frankfurter, author of the Court's opinion in both *Colegrove* and *Gomillion,* distinguished the two cases on several bases. First, the earlier decision involved the dilution of voting strength as a result of legislative inaction, while the later case claimed a denial of the right to vote as a result of positive action by the state. Second, the Alabama case involved claims of racial discrimination in violation of the Fifteenth Amendment: While the Court would not interfere with matters of a purely political nature, the Court would not allow a state to use its legitimate powers to circumvent federally protected rights. ". . . [T]hese considerations," in Frankfurter's opinion, "lift this controversy [racial gerrymander] out of the so-called political arena and into the conventional sphere of constitutional litigation."

Technically, a litigant such as WMCA could not consider *Gomillion* v. *Lightfoot* a precedent in cases of political malapportionment. *Gomillion* involved racial considerations; the malapportionment in New York was strictly a result of political factors. *Gomillion* violated the Fifteenth Amendment's proscription of denial of the right to vote on racial grounds; WMCA would have to convince the Court that the New York apportionment violated the Fourteenth Amendment's prescription of equal protection of the laws for all people. As a practical matter, however, a prospective litigant would realize that the pressure on the Court to extend its ruling to political malapportionments would be great. To those not versed in legal lore it seemed unreasonable that the Constitution forbade minorities to be deprived of their rights, but allowed majorities to be discriminated against.

However, the *Gomillion* decision was not the only factor justifying a belief that the Court might reverse itself and overrule or distinguish away *Colegrove* v. *Green:* The Illinois apportionment case and its ruling that courts could not decide such "political questions" had not been received well either in lower courts or in the law reviews. Supreme Court decisions on constitutional issues are final and can be altered only by the Court itself or by constitutional amendment, but a decision not in harmony with society's mores is likely to be difficult to enforce. The Supreme Court, therefore, cannot remain oblivious to criticism. Moreover, the justices are interested in criticisms of their informed constituents—the bar, the Justice Department, Congress, the lower courts, the law reviews, the law schools, and the better newspapers—for they are aware that they too can make mistakes. As Justice Jackson wittily noted: "We are not final because we are infallible, but we are infallible only because we are final."

In the late 1950's, two federal district courts took positions on apportionment cases which in the very least indicated a falling away from the *Colegrove* precedent. In *Dyer* v. *Kazuhisa Abe,* Chief Judge McLaughlin of the Federal District Court in Hawaii was faced with a challenge by a voter in the then Territory of Hawaii, who charged that the legislature had failed for fifty-five years to reapportion itself to adjust to the shifting population within the territory as required by the Organic Act of Hawaii. The judge held that the Equal Protection Clause of the Fourteenth Amendment applied to the Territory of Hawaii (the Fourteenth Amendment reads: "Nor shall any State . . . deny to any person . . . the equal protection of the laws"), that the existing apportionment was on its face discriminatory against voters of the populous Island of Oahu and was therefore unconstitutional. He got around the judicial barrier set up in *Colegrove* by correctly noting that Justice Frankfurter did not speak for a majority in holding that courts lacked jurisdiction in cases involving voting districts. The Court had split 3-1-3,* with Frankfurter, Reed, and Burton asserting that the issue was non-justiciable; Justices Black, Douglas and Murphy dissenting, stated that in their view the issue was meet for adjudication; and Justice Rutledge casting the crucial vote, agreeing with the dissenters that the issue was justiciable, but voting with the majority for dismissing the challenge on the narrow ground of lack of equity.

Even more important than the decision in the Hawaii case was the dicta (statements not binding because they are inessential to the holding of a case) McLaughlin issued. Noting the decision of the Supreme Court in the school segregation case, *Brown* v. *Board of Education,* he pointed out that "any distinction between racial and geographic discrimination is artificial and unrealistic. Both should be abolished."

* See footnote on p. 5.

Moreover, he issued a clarion call to the judiciary to take up arms.

It will be recalled that one reason Justice Frankfurter gave in *Colegrove* as justification for not taking jurisdiction was that the Court would be unable to give effective relief because it could not itself redistrict a state. The subsequent developments in *Dyer* suggested the opposite. McLaughlin ordered a reapportionment or, in the alternative, an election at-large. Congress reacted by itself ordering the reapportionment of the legislative districts. Moreover, the conclusion that politicians faced with the threat of at-large elections would be motivated to take affirmative action and reapportion is bolstered by a 1958 case, *McGraw* v. *Donovan,* which arose in the District Court of Minnesota. There a three-judge federal district court reserved decision on the issue of apportionment "until after the Legislature of the State of Minnesota has once more had an opportunity to deal with this problem, which is of vital concern to the people of the state." The legislature took the hint. It repealed the 1913 act under which the inequitable districts had been drawn and provided for reapportionment of legislative districts in the state to be effective in 1962.

Perhaps the strongest refute of Frankfurter's pessimistic prediction, however, is afforded by the Illinois case itself. Ironically, just a year after the *Colegrove* decision, the congressional districts of Illinois were revised for the first time in over forty years. According to the Governor, Dwight H. Green: "It was the threat that all of them [Congressmen] would have to run at-large . . . that finally got the job done."

The respectful, but critical, reaction in the law reviews to the Court's actions in apportionment litigation is best exemplified by a 1958 article written by Anthony Lewis for the *Harvard Law Review*. At the time, Lewis covered the Supreme Court for the New York *Times* and was widely acclaimed for the accuracy and skill with which he performed his duty. The substance of Lewis' argument was that judicial abstention in legislative districting was neither required legally nor effective practically. He examined the nature of malapportionment and its political effect on the relationship between the cities as against the states and the federal government, and concluded that Frankfurter was ignoring political realities in stating that "the remedy for unfairness in districting is to secure state legislatures that will apportion properly, or to invoke the ample powers of Congress."

In 1961, the Supreme Court itself took action which indicated to informed observers that the Court might be ready to reconsider the *Colegrove* decision. The Supreme Court agreed to hear an apportionment case from Tennessee, *Baker* v. *Carr*. The mere agreement of the Court to hear the case was, in itself, historic. Only a few years before the Court had dismissed an apportionment case from a state court challenging the identical Tennessee apportionment provisions. Another significant development was that the federal government, through the Office of the Solicitor General, filed an amicus curiae brief in favor of the appellants who sought judicial review of Tennessee's apportionment. When the Justice Department files such a "friend of the court" brief, it performs two functions. It brings to the controversy an experience and expertise that reflect the vast resources of the federal government, resources which can be approximated by only the largest of private law firms, and it informs the Court that the national government believes that the case involves some significant national concern.

Among the interested observers of the Court's agreement to review *Baker* v. *Carr* were the attorneys for WMCA. Oral argument in *Baker* was scheduled for April, only a few months after Max Gross sent his letter to WMCA urging that it bring suit. After listening to the oral argument and noting the questions the justices addressed to the contending counsel, Sand advised Straus that litigation was feasible. On May 1, 1961, WMCA filed a complaint in the Federal District Court in New York City challenging New York State apportionment on the grounds that it violated the Equal Protection Clause of the Fourteenth Amendment by giving the more populous areas fewer representatives than their numbers warranted.

2

A Case Is Begun

WMCA had decided to litigate: The question now was when and how. A memorandum dated April 13, 1961, about three weeks before WMCA filed its complaint, indicates some of the problems Sand and Gross first had to consider.

PRELIMINARY TEST—POINTS TO BE RESEARCHED

1. *The Parties.*

    A. Can WMCA, Inc. be a plantiff on the theory it is a taxpayer?
    B. *Parties Defendant.* One of the issues in *Baker* v. *Carr* raised by the defendants is that they were not the proper parties, since they did not control legislative reapportionment. Who would the proper parties be in New York State? . . . If their offices are in Albany, how to obtain venue in the Southern District?

2. *Exhaustion of State Remedies.*

    There are various state decisions challenging reapportionments. These must be studied and analyzed. One case apparently holds that a challenge must be brought promptly after the reapportionment.

    (1) Can we now challenge the 1950 apportionment after it has been in effect for nine years?
    (2) Shouldn't a federal court defer action on the grounds that a reapportionment will take place in the near future and it is not certain that the reapportionment will be an unfair one?

        (i) In this regard, can it be demonstrated that the apportionments undertaken in 1940 and 1950 made only insignificant changes not reflecting the population shifts revealed by the federal census? Can it be argued that past history and the composition of the present legislature is sufficient to warrant the conclusion that the 1960 reapportionment will not correct the disparities? The 1960 census figures by district and the time table for reapportionment should be obtained.

(ii) Could the imminent reapportionment be turned to our advantage on the theory that the Federal Court could retain jurisdiction over the case and hold it in abeyance to re-examine the allegations of the complaint in the light of the new reapportionment? (I take it that, for the political and public relations impact of the case, decision by the Federal Court stating that it would withhold action solely on the grounds that a state reapportionment was about to take place which might be a fair one, or if unfair, which might be limited by the state courts, would be a worthwhile accomplishment. Copies of the complaints, briefs and opinion distributed to the state legislators might produce results not otherwise obtainable. Similar events occurred in Minnesota and New Jersey, where reapportionment took place not because of a court edict but because of the influence which the pendency of the litigation had upon the legislature.)

(3) An analysis of the census figures of the 1960 census should be made and perhaps some charts prepared showing the disparity and the failure to correct in the 1940 and 1950 reapportionments. 1960 census applied to formula—what are results if legislature complies in the best of faith with formula in constitution?

(4) What remedy do we suggest—revise county lines?

The problem of standing* was solved simply and logically. Personnel at radio station WMCA were asked if they wished to be plaintiffs and one volunteer from each borough of the city was chosen to serve, together with R. Peter Straus and WMCA as the parties' plaintiff. The defendants were those state officials who had any role in administering or enforcing the election and districting laws. These included some officials of New York City and Nassau County whom

* In order to bring suit, a plaintiff must show that he is personally injured by the defendant's action.

WMCA had hoped would join the plaintiffs in opposing New York's apportionment. The radio station had good reason to be optimistic in this respect: John English, Nassau County Democratic leader, successfully petitioned the Supreme Court for leave to file an amicus curiae brief on behalf of a group of Nassau County voters, showing the possible impact of the *Baker* case on Nassau County.

WMCA was determined to proceed with its suit as rapidly as possible. The radio station realized that if it waited until *Baker* v. *Carr* was decided, it might lose the opportunity to be the first to bring legal action successfully challenging New York State's apportionment. Considerable interest and public discussion were anticipated and WMCA was anxious to share the publicity. Filing too soon, however, carried equally grave risks. As WMCA attorney Leonard Sand recalls: "On May 1, 1961, our complaint was complete and I took it to the United States Courthouse on Foley Square for filing. May 1 was also a Monday on which the Supreme Court was announcing opinions. Out of what I thought was an excess of caution, I telephoned the office of the Clerk of the Supreme Court to see if any decision had been rendered in *Baker* v. *Carr*. We would have looked very foolish if we had started an apportionment case on the same day that the Supreme Court had said that such suits could not be brought." As it turned out, that very day the Court set *Baker* down for reargument in October.

If WMCA hoped for publicity, it certainly had no cause for disappointment. Stories were carried by all major newspapers as well as the more specialized media which report on the entertainment world. Representative of the latter was an article printed in *Variety,* which emphasized the radio station's tradition of active editorializing on public matters and its role as a public servant.

WMCA, as a radio station, of course, had unique opportunities to propagandize. The day after the suit was filed, President Straus took to the air to rally support for his cause.

> There are twenty-five counties in upstate New York which together have barely a third the population of Brooklyn, but they cast more votes than Brooklyn in the New York State Assembly.
>
> Why? Because seats in both houses of the New York State Legis-

lature are assigned throughout the state under a formula which favors upstate New York over New York City.

WMCA is doing something about it. This week WMCA filed a suit in Federal Court aimed at winning more equal representation for all voters in the state.

If you would like to join the fight, send a card to Equal Vote, WMCA, New York 17. . . . Give *your* support to this campaign to make *your* vote as good as the vote of New Yorkers upstate.

Nor did WMCA restrict its attempt to rally support to the impersonal means of radio broadcasts. Letters were sent to such potentially interested civic organizations as the American Civil Liberties Union, the League of Women Voters, the Association of the Bar of New York City, the Twentieth Century Fund, and the National Municipal League. Individuals contacted included Herbert Lehman, Eleanor Roosevelt and David Rockefeller, as well as prominent city and state politicians including New York City Mayor Robert Wagner, Congressman John Lindsay, Newbold Morris, Robert Moses, and Senators Jacob Javits and Kenneth Keating.

While WMCA was handling publicity, attorneys Leonard Sand and Max Gross were confronting difficult obstacles even in getting a hearing for their case. The first thing they had to do was to convince Federal District Judge Richard H. Levet that his court had jurisdiction; that is, that some federal statute granted to the court the authority to hear cases of this nature. They relied on the Civil Rights Act of 1960 and the Federal Declaratory Judgment Act. The Civil Rights Act grants to any person who has been deprived by state action of any right, privilege or immunity secured by the Constitution or federal law, the right to a trial in a federal district court. WMCA claimed it was denied the right of the equal protection of the laws, guaranteed by the Fourteenth Amendment. The Federal Declaratory Judgment Act empowered the court to state the rights of the respective parties to the suit.

WMCA also sought to persuade Judge Levet to convene a three-judge district court which would have the power to issue an interlocutory or permanent injunction restraining the action of any officer of such a state in the enforcement or execution of such a statute. In other words, in the context of this case, such a court could bar the state from holding any further elections under its present system of apportionment. Another asset of such a court is that a direct appeal from its judgment goes to the Supreme Court, bypassing the intermediate Court of Appeals. The advantage of this is to expedite the final determination of cases in which state constitutional provisions or statutes are called into question.

The problem faced by WMCA was that the single district court judge before whom the case first appears convenes a three-judge court only if a substantial question is presented. Attorneys representing New York State and Nassau, Suffolk, and Westchester Counties filed motions to dismiss the complaint. Defendant Abe Stark, president of the City Council of the City of New York, and the commissioners of the Board of Elections of the City of New York admitted all of plaintiff's allegations and asked the Court to grant the relief requested in WMCA's complaint. New York City, of course, while technically a defendant, was underrepresented in the state legislature and shared the petitioner's desire to alter the inequitable situation.

Attorney General Louis J. Lefkowitz, in his brief for the state in support of the motion to dismiss the complaint asserted that (1) the Court lacked jurisdiction over the subject matter; and (2) the complaint failed to state a claim upon which relief could be granted. His arguments were five:

POINT I

The formula for apportionment of state legislative representation is not open to constitutional challenge on the sole asserted ground that it is not in direct ratio to the population. This allegation simply serves to raise a political, nonjudiciable issue, upon which the federal courts will not grant declaratory injunctions or other relief.

POINT II

The complaint does not allege a substantial federal question. The federal laws and Constitution do not prohibit the states from adopting a system of apportionment which includes factors other than population, so long as race, sex or other criteria condemned by the Fifteenth and Nineteenth amendments are not employed.

POINT III

The action as against the state officials, being tantamount to one against the State of New York, is barred by the Eleventh Amendment* to the Constitution.

POINT IV

The corporate plaintiff [radio station WMCA] in any event lacks standing to substitute suit for the relief requested.

POINT V

The Federal Court has no power to grant the demanded relief, as it would ultimately entail an unconstitutional invasion of the doctrine of separation of powers.

WMCA did not confine its response to the Attorney General to the reply brief it filed with the Court. It also took to the air, using to good advantage the fact that Lefkowitz had political ambitions:

> The State of New York . . . through the Attorney General's office, filed a motion to dismiss our complaint. In doing so, a spokesman for the Attorney General gave not only technical reasons, but said that there's nothing at all unfair about the way New York City is short-changed on its representation in the legislature.
>
> Now who is the Attorney General whose office takes this position? He's Louis Lefkowitz, Republican candidate for the office of Mayor of New York City. If you feel, as WMCA does, that any candidate for this office should get behind the battle for *your* voting rights, let him know about it.

Straus' editorial attack elicited a quick response from Lefkowitz. In a letter dated June 14, 1961 the Attorney General accused WMCA of misrepresenting his position. He insisted that:

> As the Attorney General the law imposes upon me the duty of defending against any challenge which is addressed to the state constitu-

---

* "The judicial power of the United States shall not be construed to extend to any suit in law or equity, commenced or prosecuted against one of the United States by citizens of another state, or by citizens or subjects of any foreign state"—Eleventh Amendment.

tion or a state statute. My personal opinion as to the wisdom or·fair-
ness of the constitutional provision or statute under attack in this
court is immaterial and of no consequence.

On June 7, 1961, the trial on the motion to convene a three-judge
court began before the Honorable Richard H. Levet, district judge.
As Levet immediately made clear, he was quite familiar with all the
materials filed by the litigants. What he did wish was information in
answer to seven specific questions.

> *Judge Levet:* I am going to ask the plaintiff to argue the matter
> first . . . and then I shall of course permit the defendants to speak
> on the motion to dismiss and, if necessary, I shall give the plaintiffs
> a right to answer the defendants' arguments.
>
> In your discussion, Mr. Sand, I wish you will cover the following
> issues:
>
> First, what do the plaintiffs seek in the complaint, what is the relief
> demanded;
>
> Secondly, what is the basis of federal jurisdiction;
>
> Thirdly, what are the constitutional rights of the plaintiffs, if any,
> which are impaired;
>
> Fourthly, what the plaintiffs seek on this motion;
>
> Fifthly, does this Court with one judge have the right to consider
> dismissal;
>
> Sixthly, what basis, if any, is there for the consideration of the af-
> fidavits, particularly that of the professor;
>
> Seventh and last, what Supreme Court authority is there for this ac-
> tion in view of the parent determinations emanating from that hon-
> able Court?

After a brief discussion of the reasons for convening a three-judge
court, the attorneys came to a more controversial issue, the effect
which a court order enjoining elections would have on state government.

> *Mr. Sand:* The relief which the plaintiffs seek . . . is that the de-
> fendants be enjoined . . . from performing those particular duties
> which [they have] with respect to election laws.

The Court: What kind of a vacuum does that leave?

Mr. Sand: If your Honor please, I respectfully suggest that it leaves no vacuum.

The Court: Who rushes in to determine how the apportionments are to be made?

Mr. Sand: The specific relief requested is that after the Court issues a declaration of invalidity, that it retain jurisdiction of this case as did other federal courts in similar matters.

. . .

The Court: Then you contemplate this Court in that instance should supervise the plan which is substituted for the present plan under the Constitution of the State of New York?

. . .

If there is not a plan substituted which is acceptable to this Court under your proposal of continuing jurisdiction, there will be no election, is that so? Or, in that event, you might have no election in 1961 or 1962, as far as that is concerned?

Mr. Sand: I think it is relevant to the timing of this action and why it was brought at this time that there is no state-wide election until 1962, so there will be ample time for the legislature to take corrective action.

The Court: Could the legislature do this alone?

Mr. Sand: Not alone.

The Court: So what would have to be done? A special constitutional convention?

Mr. Sand: There is no requirement that the apportionment of the legislature be by a constitutional provision. Once this Court strikes from the constitution the apportionment provisions, then the New York State Legislature—

The Court: Can you say to the legislature to substitute its own no matter what the voters of the State of New York think?

Mr. Sand: I take it what the legislature would do would be to enact an interim apportionment provision and also propose a constitutional amendment, because I take it the people of New York desire to have the matter of the apportionment of their legislature contained in the state constitution. However, there is no necessity that that be the case.

The Court: In other words, you say that this Court would have the

power to strike right out of the state constitution the provisions with
respect to apportionment for Assemblymen and Senators?

Mr. Sand: Just as other federal courts have stricken from other
state constitutions—

The Court: At least that is your position?

Mr. Sand: Yes.

The next significant exchange arose over the question of what
standards the Fourteenth Amendment imposed on state apportionments. WMCA emphasized the disparities in population of upstate
and urban areas having equal representation, arguing that the courts
obviously would disallow a provision of a state constitution which
said that every citizen residing in an urban area would have one-half
a vote or one-tenth a vote, and every citizen residing in a rural area
would have a full vote or two votes. This statement prompted the
following:

> *The Court:* I assume you are familiar with some of the Michigan
> statutes which provide for a 30 per cent basis on territory and a 70
> per cent on population. . . . Is there anything wrong with that un-
> der the Fourteenth Amendment?
>
> *Mr. Sand:* Under the Fourteenth Amendment it is permissible for
> a state to adopt a fair and rational system of representation.
>
> *The Court:* As you phrase it, what do you mean by "fair and ra-
> tional"? What is fair and rational to you may not be to another. I
> happen to have lived near Yates County at one time, they may feel
> very definite about the necessity of an Assemblyman from the
> county in order to care for their geographical rights.
>
> *Mr. Sand:* It is not the position of the plaintiff that there need be in
> both houses of the legislature a precise or mathematical proportion to
> population. But it is the position of the plaintiff that in a bicameral
> legislature which represents the people, as does the New York State
> Constitution, that there must be a fair and rational basis in at least
> one of the two houses between population and representation.

Irving Galt, assistant solicitor general and attorney for the State
of New York, reiterated the arguments made in Lefkowitz's brief
and emerged relatively unscathed by Judge Levet's questions. Assistant Corporation Counsel Handel, appearing for defendants Abe

Stark and the Board of Elections of the City of New York, was less fortunate, as is clear from the following:

> *Mr. Handel:* . . . [W]e have suggested in our brief, and I repeat with deference, rather than determining the issue at this time that it might be well for your Honor to adjourn these motions until the Supreme Court has at least given its decision in the *Baker* case. [Tennessee apportionment case]
>
> *The Court:* I haven't very good cold storage facilities.
>
> *Mr. Handel:* . . . It is largely an exercise in futility to go through all the procedures at this time at least until we obtain the guidance of the Supreme Court.
>
> *The Court:* If you did that, we might have a vast accumulation of backlog which would be somewhat difficult to supervise. I expect if possible to decide this case as rapidly as I can one way or the other. I am not particularly amenable, I must say, to the doctrine of delay.

True to his word, the judge did proceed quite rapidly. On July 7, 1961, exactly a month after hearing oral arguments, Levet delivered his opinion. An examination of Supreme Court decisions, he noted, revealed that despite the language used by Justice Frankfurter in *Colegrove* v. *Green,* the Illinois apportionment case, a majority of the justices had never expressly held that the Court was without jurisdiction over matters concerning legislative apportionment, whether on a national or state level. Moreover, he continued: "That this Court should disclaim jurisdiction because the question presented touches upon an area denominated as 'political' is not sufficiently persuasive, in my opinion, to preclude judicial entertainment and consideration of such issues. The Supreme Court has not refrained from determinations of controversies involving political aspects when a right to judicial relief has been established and deemed appropriate." Therefore, he concluded, "the issues presented herein are of such a character as to warrant the convening of a three-judge court."

WMCA had won the first round.

On July 20, 1961, the Court of Appeals for the Second Circuit (New York, Connecticut and Vermont) designated Sterry R. Waterman, Sylvester J. Ryan and Richard H. Levet as the three judges who would hear WMCA's case. Waterman was a judge on the Court of

Appeals; Ryan, the chief judge of the District Court and Levet, of course, the judge who had convened the special statutory court. Argument was set for November.

A new element entered the case when on November 6, Eugene H. Nickerson petitioned the court for leave to join the action as either an intervenor or amicus curiae in support of the plaintiffs. Nickerson, the Democratic party's victorious candidate for the office of County Executive of Nassau County had indicated interest in WMCA's suit as early as July when he wrote a letter to the New York *Times* castigating the legislature for its refusal to reform the apportionment system in New York. His victory as the first Democrat ever elected to the office of Nassau County Executive caused the county to switch positions and support WMCA's appeal. Moreover, in February, 1962, the County Board of Supervisors, although still controlled by Republicans, recognized the shift in political sentiment represented by November's vote and, reversing its position of the previous March, passed a resolution directing the legislators from Nassau to work in Albany for a constitutional amendment increasing the county's representation.

Oral argument before Judges Waterman, Levet, and Ryan began on November 15, 1961. The question the statutory court was considering was *not* whether New York's apportionment system was inequitable, but rather whether the issue of apportionment was justiciable and could be determined by the Court. After some preliminary skirmishing over such technical matters as whether Nassau County Executive Eugene Nickerson could enter the case as an intervenor or an amicus curiae (the Court decided in favor of the latter), the argument swiftly moved to a head as Judge Levet asked Leonard Sand, attorney for WMCA, how he thought the Fourteenth Amendment guaranteed districts of equal population to voters.

> *Mr. Sand:* Well, I think the Fourteenth Amendment guarantees— it guarantees due process and equal protection coupled with the guarantees—
> *Judge Levet:* Where do you arrive at that from?
> *Mr. Sand:* I beg—
> *Judge Levet:* On voters, as to the number of persons in a district, how is that derived in your thought?

Mr. Sand: I think, I respectfully submit, that it is derived from the concept that embodied in that amendment is a system of government in which the representatives of the people govern by the consent of the governed and that if a legislature is empowered to act for the state by virtue of an elective system which is not representative of the people and if, as we further allege, that legislature so conducts itself in a manner which is discriminatory towards the unrepresented elements of the population, there is then a denial of due process and equal protection of the laws.

Judge Levet: Then, how do you account for the statement in the per curiam opinion in *MacDougall* v. *Green* as follows:

"To assume that political power is a function exclusively of numbers is to disregard the practicalities of government. Thus the Constitution protects the interest of the smaller against the greater by giving in the Senate, for example, entirely unequal representation of populations. . . ."

Mr. Sand: Well, if your Honor please, *MacDougall* is also an eve of election case, a case in which the Court was powerless to grant any relief which would have been effective prior to the election for which those nominating petitions were designed.

I think that with respect to questions of nomination, the wish of a state to have geographical areas have a greater voice than with respect to the actual election—

Judge Levet: Why—

Mr. Sand: I think—because at the ensuing election, the popular vote will be heard. . . .

I want to make it very clear, as I perhaps have not yet done in oral argument, that the plaintiffs by no means contend that the constitution requires that both houses of a bicameral legislature represent in exact mathematical proportion the population. We make no such contention, but we do say this: That where you have a bicameral legislature, as in New York, and where the constitution says that the districts shall be as nearly as may be equal in population and so there is no purported attempt to have apportionment based on tax revenue or land holdings, or anything of that sort: Where you have such a situation and where in both houses of the legislature there is a gross disproportion between population and representation, then at least the

burden shifts, the burden shifts upon the proponents of that scheme
of government to come forward and to defend it, but that where such
a situation exists, at least a cause of action is stated and the matter
should be heard.

Not surprisingly, Irving Galt, appearing as attorney for the State
of New York, offered a different view of what factors the state should
take into account in fashioning an apportionment scheme. Perhaps
recalling WMCA's editorial attack on Lefkowitz (he was defeated
by Robert Wagner, a Democrat, in his bid for the office of Mayor
of New York City), Galt first hastened to assure the Court that the
views he were expressing were not necessarily his own:

> *Mr. Galt:* Now again, may I say this to the Court, so that there
> will be no misunderstanding as to the Attorney General's position: We
> are here in our position as the legal officer of the state, customarily
> coming before the Court to defend the constitutionality of statutes.
> We have no personal opinion which we wish to express to the Court
> as to the wisdom or lack of wisdom, the fairness or the unfairness
> of the particular legislation, or the constitutional provisions out of
> which it arises.
>
> We simply say that the question here is whether, assuming that
> there are sufficient facts otherwise set forth, whether there can be
> any possibility that the Fourteenth Amendment of the Constitution
> in anywise could have been violated by the sixty or seventy years of
> apportionment which have taken place since the founding constitu-
> tional provisions in 1894.
>
> Now, to begin with, I think I should be very clearly understood
> . . . that with respect to both houses, insofar as New York is con-
> cerned, the underlying theory is that population is a prime factor,
> or the prime factor, but that geographical and territorial considera-
> tions, mostly as embodied by the traditional county lines, are also taken
> into account. This is the underlying rationale of New York [State]
> constitutional and statutory legislation with respect to apportionment.

Galt then went on to challenge the right of the Court to assume
jurisdiction. In his view, "it is in a sense hostile to the democratic
process for the courts to intrude themselves . . . into the realm of

the people's politics." This statement elicited sharp response from the Court:

> *Judge Levet:* I would like to have you state again: Why should not the Court consider the case on its merits with respect to whether or not this situation which exists, at least inferentially here, is or is not a violation of the Fourteenth Amendment.
> *Mr. Galt:* All right.
> *Judge Levet:* In other words, why can it be said that merely because it is political, in substance that therefore [it] is sacred? In other words, what is there which gives some "sacred cow" attitude to a political situation, if that is so?

•　　•　　•

> *Mr. Galt:* To do this, to intervene in a case of this kind for the Court I think would mean this: It would mean a substitution of the Court's judgment in this case particularly has been exercised in accordance with historical tradition and as, for instance, in accordance with other things that denominate how a democracy like ours functions.

The final point in which the Court seemed interested was if there was any evidence as to whether New York's apportionment reflected the wishes of the people:

> *Judge Levet:* It has been twice approved and approved by the people, is that correct, 1894 and 1938?
> *Mr. Galt:* Right. The people themselves did not wish, as I recall it in 1958,* to have a constitutional convention again.
> *Judge Levet:* Well, in 1938 they must have approved this form of apportionment, is that so?
> *Mr. Galt:* That is right; that is correct. . . .

On January 10, 1962, an article in the New York *Times* reported that the Democrats would attempt to alter New York's apportionment system.

---

* A referendum concerning a constitutional convention was held in 1957.

DEMOCRATS SEEK TO REAPPORTION SEATS IN ALBANY

Amendment Is Asked to End
Unequal Representation
for Populous Counties

BY DOUGLAS DALES

ALBANY, Jan. 9—Democrats will concentrate at the 1962 legislative session on obtaining the first passage of a constitutional amendment reversing the formulas for apportioning Senate and Assembly seats.

•   •   •

Joseph Zaretzki, the Senate minority leader, declared at a news conference today that the present formulas, based partly on conditions prevailing in 1894, had created "a Boston Tea Party situation—taxation without representation."

•   •   •

Formula Is Cited

Under the present formula, he (Zaretzki) said, the six largest counties, with a total population of 9,519,316, would have twenty-six Senate seats and the fifty-six remaining counties, with a population of 6,721,470, would have thirty-one seats. The six largest are Brooklyn, Manhattan, the Bronx, Queens, Nassau and Erie.

Senator Zaretzki cited Nassau and Suffolk as offering a "glaring example" of unequal representation under the present formula. Both counties would have three Senators, but Nassau's population is 1,300,-171, compared with 666,784 for Suffolk.

The Democratic bill, still being drafted, will propose a Senate of sixty seats and an Assembly of 180. There are now fifty-eight seats in the Senate and 150 in the Assembly.

Senate districts would be composed of areas of equal population, regardless of county lines. There would be three Assembly seats of equal size in each Senate district.

Revision of apportionment formulas topped a list of Democratic legislative objectives announced today by Senator Zaretzki and Anthony J. Travia, the Assembly Democratic leader.

The following day, January 11, the three-man statutory court unleashed a thunderbolt. In three separate opinions, Judges Levet, Waterman and Ryan unanimously rejected WMCA's complaint.

The principal opinion was delivered by Judge Levet. He considered in turn three issues: jurisdiction; the question of the sufficiency of the complaint; and the matter of want of equity and justiciability. Levet began by examining Supreme Court precedents in apportionment cases and concluded: "The United States Supreme Court never held that the federal courts were without jurisdiction over matters concerning legislative apportionment involving either congressional or state legislative apportionments. Rather, it appears that the Court has seen fit in specific instances to decline to exercise its equity power in that area." He thus rejected the argument of the New York State Attorney General that *Colegrove* was a barrier to judicial inspection of apportionments. In the judge's opinion, *Colegrove* v. *Green,* the Illinois apportionment case, turned on the question of want of equity.

In considering the sufficiency of WMCA's complaint, Levet accepted as admitted the disparities in citizen population necessitated by the provisions of New York State's Constitution: However, he stated: "There is no authoritative indication that the relative weight accorded individual votes in elections for the state legislature . . . is protected by the Equal Protection Clause of the Fourteenth Amendment. In fact, the contrary seems true." Moreover, in *MacDougall* v. *Green,* the 1948 Illinois case involving state requirements for filing of petitions in primaries, the Supreme Court held, in a per curiam opinion (a brief, unsigned order of the Court):

> *To assume that political power is a function exclusively of numbers is to disregard the practicalities of government.* Thus, the Constitution protects the interests of the smaller against the greater by giving in the Senate entirely unequal representation to populations. It would be strange indeed, and doctrinaire, for this Court, applying such broad constitutional concepts as due process and equal protection of the laws, to deny a state the power to assure a proper diffusion of political initiative as between its thinly populated counties and those having concentrated masses, in view of the fact that the latter have practical opportunities for exerting their political weight at the polls not available to the former. The Constitution—a practical instrument of government—makes no such demands on the states.

For these reasons, Levet continued, "I . . . find that the complaint fails to state a claim upon which relief can be granted and, accordingly, it must be dismissed."

Judge Levet's third point was that there was want of equity and lack of justiciability. As Justice Rutledge pointed out in his concurring opinion in *Colegrove:* "The power of a court of equity to act is a discretionary one. . . . Where a federal court of equity is asked to interfere with the enforcement of state laws, it should do so only to prevent irreparable injury which is clear and imminent." In Levet's view, for a federal court to interfere with a state's constitutional provisions in regard to apportionment would initiate "a far-reaching revision of federal-state relationships." Obviously, he concluded: "The inherent impracticabilities of such a course demonstrate the want of equity or justiciability in such a procedure."

Judge Ryan, in his concurring opinion, agreed with Levet that the Court had jurisdiction to entertain the suit and that the complaint should be dismissed on its merits. He rejected WMCA's argument that the New York apportionment was analogous with the situation existing in *Gomillion* v. *Lightfoot.** In marked contrast, Judge Ryan pointed out:

> There is no claim made here that the apportionment formula before us or the laws enacted to apply it effect a discrimination against any particular racial or religious group. The complaint is that the method of apportionment gives rise solely to territorial or purely geographical boundaries affecting the right of suffrage can not be supported by mere territorial discrimination and nothing more.

Judge Waterman, in his concurring opinion, mildly rebuked Levet and Ryan for deciding too much:

> My colleagues deny relief after having taken jurisdiction of the case. I do not quarrel directly with them, but because I believe this litigation is not justiciable, I think it appropriate to point out the admonition of Mr. Justice Frankfurter relative to "jurisdiction" stated by him in *Colegrove:* "We are of the opinion that the petitioners ask of this Court what is beyond its competence to grant. This is one of those demands on judicial power which cannot be met by verbal

* It will be recalled that in that case the Supreme Court struck down an apportionment of the Alabama State Legislature designed to remove all Negro voters from the boundaries of the City of Tuskegee.

fencing about 'jurisdiction.' It must be resolved by considerations on the basis of which this Court, from time to time, has refused to do so because due regard for the effective working of our government revealed this issue to be of a peculiarly political nature and therefore not meet for judicial determination."

At radio station WMCA, the reaction to the Court's decision was one of disappointment, but not discouragement. As stated by President R. Peter Straus, WMCA "took a licking in court," but did not intend to let the matter drop. On February 5, attorneys Sand and Gross appealed the statutory court's decision directly to the United States Supreme Court, in accordance with the provisions of the Federal Code of Civil Procedure.

3

Baker v. *Carr:*
A Judicial Landmark

New hope for the *WMCA* case came quickly. On Monday, March 26, 1962, the Supreme Court handed down its judgment in *Baker* v. *Carr*. In a 6-2 decision, with no less than six written opinions, the Supreme Court held that federal courts have jurisdiction over apportionment controversies; that the issue is justiciable; and that voters have standing to challenge state apportionments.

The principal opinion of the Court was delivered by 56-year-old Justice William J. Brennan. He was joined in the majority by Chief Justice Earl Warren, 71; Justice Hugo Black, 76; Justice Tom C. Clark, 63; Justice William O. Douglas, 64; and Justice Potter Stewart, 47. Clark, Douglas, and Stewart wrote separate concurring opinions. Justice Felix Frankfurter, 80, and Justice John Marshall Harlan, 63, dissented. Justice Charles Whittaker did not participate.*

Justice William Brennan was the only Roman Catholic on the Court. A graduate of Harvard Law School, he was in private practice from 1931 to 1949, when he became a New Jersey Superior Court judge. The following year he was promoted to the Appellate Division and in 1952 became a justice of the Supreme Court of New Jersey. Although a Democrat, Brennan was appointed to the Supreme Court by Republican President Dwight Eisenhower in 1956. The only justice who had extensive experience on the bench before becoming a member of the Supreme Court, Brennan has become identified with the "activist" wing of the Court. In general, he has taken "liberal" positions on both economic and civil liberties issues.

Brennan began by stating the facts of the case. The appellants had

* Ages are given as of the time of the decision.

filed a class suit (in a class suit, the plaintiff sues not only in behalf of his own rights, but also in behalf of all those similarly situated; e.g., a Negro charging that he is denied his Fourteenth Amendment right to equal protection of the laws by a state policy of school segregation is fighting not only for the right of his children to attend integrated schools, but also the right of all Negroes to send their children to such schools) complaining that they were denied the equal protection of the laws by virtue of the debasement of their votes. The action was brought under the Civil Rights Act, which prohibits states from depriving people of any rights, privileges or immunities secured by the Constitution or federal statutes.

The Constitution of the State of Tennessee required that a census be taken every ten years and that the legislature be apportioned according to the number of qualified voters in each county. These provisions were complied with from 1871 to 1901 when the Tennessee General Assembly adopted its present apportionment act. In the following sixty years all attempts to reapportion failed. As a result of changes as the state's population grew from two million to three and one-half million, the relative standings of the counties in terms of qualified voters was altered significantly.

The first question Brennan thought must be answered was whether the courts have jurisdiction over state apportionments. Article III of the United States Constitution provides that "the judicial power shall extend to all cases, in law and equity, arising under this Constitution, the laws of the United States, and treaties made, or which shall be made, under their authority. . . ." By complaining of a deprivation of Fourteenth Amendment rights, the plaintiffs had set forth a case "arising under" the Constitution. Supreme Court decisions offered precedents for sustaining the federal courts' jurisdiction over subjects of this kind. *Colegrove* was not a barrier: The three dissenters, accompanied by Justice Rutledge, had all held that the courts had jurisdiction over apportionments; since only seven justices participated in the decision, these four constituted a majority of the Court on that issue.

The second matter Justice Brennan considered was the question of the standing of the appellants to challenge Tennessee's apportionment. Only when it is called upon to adjudge the legal rights of litigants in actual controversies may a federal court adjudicate the constitutionality of any statute. One cannot challenge the constitutionality of a law merely because one thinks it inequitable; the litigant must prove that he is personally injured by the law. For example, a white man cannot challenge a law discriminating against Negroes because the law does not affect him personally, even if it offends his sense of equality.

The complaint was filed by qualified voters of the state's most populous counties. They claimed to be injured personally in that Tennessee's apportionment disfavored the voters in the counties in which they resided, placing them in a position of constitutionally unjustifiable inequality vis-à-vis voters in less populous counties.

The third and most important question for the Court to consider was whether the complaint raised a justiciable issue, or, to put the question more specifically, whether a state's apportionment was a political question not meet for adjudication. After an exhaustive review of Supreme Court decisions in the areas of foreign relations, the validity of enactments, the status of Indian tribes, and the determination of whether a state possessed a republican form of government, Justice Brennan issued an authoritative definition of the nature of a political question:

> Prominent on the surface of any case held to involve a political question is found a textually demonstrable constitutional commitment of the issue to a coordinate political department; or a lack of judicially discoverable and manageable standards for resolving it; or the impossibility of deciding without an initial policy determination of a kind clearly for nonjudicial discretion; or the impossibility of a court's undertaking independent resolution without expressing lack of respect due coordinate branches of government; or an unusual need for unquestioning adherence to a political decision already made; or the potentiality of embarrassment from multifarious pronouncements by various departments on one question.

Moreover, Justice Brennan concluded, the apportionment of legislative bodies fall under none of these categories.

Justice Douglas, while joining in the opinion of the Court, felt that "a word of explanation" was necessary.

Justice William O. Douglas is a graduate of Columbia Law School and while working as a Wall Street lawyer ("to view the natives," he says), he taught law at Columbia. Douglas then joined the Yale Law School faculty and became known as one of the leading exponents of legal realism, a school of thought which emphasized concentration on what judges actually did, rather than what they said they did. Among the many government positions Douglas held, most important was the chairmanship of the Securities and Exchange Commission. He was appointed to the Supreme Court by President Franklin D. Roosevelt in 1939. A prolific author, he has written numerous books on such diverse subjects as mountain climbing, his travels in foreign countries, the law of India, and most important, American constitutional law. Along with Justice Black, Douglas occupies what most consider the extreme leftwing of the Court. An ardent liberal, he has consistently voted to protect the rights of men from infringement by government action.

In his concurring opinion, Douglas insisted that he was not deciding on the merits of the case, that is, whether Tennessee's apportionment was fair; but he did indicate that in his view the test by which the courts should determine whether a state has violated the Equal Protection Clause of the Fourteenth Amendment is whether the state has made "an invidious discrimination." While he denied that universal equality of voters is necessary ("there is room for weighting"), he stated that if it could be proved that voting disparities in Tennessee were as much as 19:1, "a case for relief [would be] established."

A second concurring opinion was written by Justice Clark. Tom C. Clark is a graduate of the University of Texas Law School. Of all members of the Court, Clark has had the most experience as a government attorney (he is colloquially called, "the prosecutor on the Court"). He served as a civil district attorney in Dallas County, Texas, as an assistant attorney general in both the antitrust and criminal divisions of the Department of Justice, and from 1945-49, as Attorney General of the United States. Appointed to the Supreme Court by President Harry S Truman in 1949, Clark is firmly entrenched in the conservative wing of the Court. He is particularly noted for his position that law enforcement officers must be given extensive powers to enable them to combat rising crime rates and to maintain the nation's internal security.

Justice Clark, who does not subscribe to the opinion that judicial propriety means that judges must speak only in measured, restrained, dignified tones, began by castigating the Court for its timidness and his colleagues for the confusing nature of their opinions:

> One emerging from the rash of opinions with their accompanying clashing of views may well find himself suffering a mental blindness. The Court holds that the appellants have alleged a cause of action. However, it refuses to award relief here—although the facts are undisputed—and fails to give the District Court any guidance whatever.

On the basis of the information available in the record, Justice Clark determined that 37% of the voters of Tennessee elected twenty of the thirty-three Senators while 40% of the voters elected sixty-three of the ninety-nine members of the House. Moreover, the frequency and magnitude of the inequities did not even reflect a definite policy. Rather, to use Clark's colorful phrase, Tennessee's apportionment was "a crazy quilt" without rational basis.

Clark next came to the point which was for him crucial: Judicial intervention was the only way in which the discrimination could be rectified:

> Although I find the Tennessee apportionment statute offends the Equal Protection Clause, I would not consider intervention by this Court into so delicate a field if there were any other relief available to the people of Tennessee. But the majority of the people of Tennessee have no "practical opportunities for exerting their political weight at the polls" to correct the existing "invidious discrimination." Tennessee has no initiative and referendum. . . . It is said that there is recourse in Congress and perhaps that may be, but from a practical standpoint this is without substance. To date Congress has never undertaken such a task in any state. We therefore must conclude that the people of Tennessee are stymied and without judicial intervention will be saddled with the present discrimination in the affairs of their state government.

The final concurring opinion was filed by Justice Stewart. Potter Stewart is a graduate of the Yale Law School and was a fellow at Cambridge University. He was in private practice first in New York City and later in Cincinnati, Ohio. Stewart was appointed by President Eisenhower in 1954 to the Court of Appeals for the Sixth Circuit and then to the Supreme Court in 1958. On the bench, Stewart has taken a moderately conservative position.

Stewart, concerned that the numerous separate opinions might confuse what the Court had in fact decided, emphasized the limited effect of the decision. The Court had merely held that the courts have jurisdiction, the issue was justiciable, and the appellants lack standing to sue. No view, he pointed out, should be thought to have been expressed on the merits of the case.

The first of the two dissenting opinions was filed by Justice Frankfurter. Felix Frankfurter was both the only Jewish and foreign-born (Vienna) member of the Court. A graduate of Harvard Law School, he became known as a brilliant legal scholar and devoted adviser to Franklin D. Roosevelt during the twenty-five years he taught law at Harvard. At the time he was appointed to the Supreme Court by President Roosevelt (1939), Frankfurter was considered an extreme liberal: As co-founder and contributing editor of *The New Republic,* he had frequently championed liberal causes, particularly the rights of Negroes. On the Court (he retired in August, 1962; thus *Baker* v. *Carr* was one of the last cases he considered), he was best-known for his emphasis on judicial restraint. Ideologically, Frankfurter must be considered a conservative.

Frankfurter, who was joined in his dissent by Justice Harlan, began by asserting that the Court was disregarding precedents (mostly, opinions such as *Colegrove* which he himself had written) and endangering the power of the judiciary by usurping power and disregarding the practical limits to judicial action:

> . . . *Disregard of inherent limits in the effective exercise of the Court's "judicial Power" not only presages the futility of judicial intervention in the essentially political conflict of forces by which the relation between population and representation has time out of mind*

been and now is determined. It may well impair the Court's position
as the ultimate organ of "the supreme law of the land" in that vast
range of legal problems, often strongly entangled in popular feeling,
on which this Court must pronounce. The Court's authority—possessed
neither of the purse nor the sword—ultimately rests on sustained public
confidence in its moral sanction. Such feeling must be nourished by
the Court's complete detachment, in fact and appearance, from politi-
cal entanglements and by abstention from injecting itself into the clash
*of political forces in political settlements.**

A second dissenting opinion, in which Frankfurter joined, was
filed by Justice Harlan.

John Marshall Harlan is the grandson of Justice John Marshall
Harlan, who was best noted for his spirited dissents in favor of the
power of the federal government to legislate to protect the Negro
under the provisions of the Civil War amendments. A Rhodes
Scholar (Balliol College, Oxford) and a graduate of New York
School of Law, Harlan worked as an assistant attorney for the United
States and then for the attorney general's office of New York State before joining a Wall Street law firm. He was appointed by President
Eisenhower to the Court of Appeals for the Second Circuit in 1954
and to the Supreme Court the following year. Closely identified with
Justice Frankfurter, Harlan has preached judicial restraint and has
advocated allowing the states considerable freedom to manage their
own affairs.

Harlan stated outright that, even if all of the appellants' allegations
were considered to be true, Tennessee had not denied them of any
rights assured by the Fourteenth Amendment.

> . . . [T]here is nothing in the federal Constitution to prevent a state,
> acting not irrationally, from choosing any electoral legislative structure
> it thinks best suited to the interests, temper, and customs of its
> people. . . . A state's choice to distribute electoral strength among
> geographical units, rather than according to a census of population,
> is certainly no less a rational decision of policy than would be its
> choice to levy a tax on property rather than a tax on income. Both are
> legislative judgments entitled to equal respect from this Court.

* Author's italics.

Due to the plethora of conflicting opinions it was difficult to determine precisely what the Court had decided and what would be the effect of its determination upon the law of apportionment. What could be confidently predicted, however, was that the lower courts would be quite uncertain as to how to try apportionment conflicts on their merits. The Supreme Court had refused to establish standards by which the Fourteenth Amendment could be imposed on state apportionments.

Justice Brennan, who delivered the principal decision, had been quite brief, to say the least, in offering guidance to the lower courts:

> Judicial standards under the Equal Protection Clause are well developed and familiar, and it has been open to courts since the enactment of the Fourteenth Amendment to determine, if on the particular facts they must, that a determination reflects *no* policy, but simply arbitrary and capricious action.

If possible, Justice Douglas was even less helpful. In his concurring opinion he merely stated, in an offhand manner, that "any relief accorded can be fashioned in the light of well-known principles of equity."

Immediate reaction to the Supreme Court's decision in *Baker* v. *Carr* was generally favorable. President John F. Kennedy gave unqualified endorsement to its underlying principle: "Quite obviously," he said, "the right to fair representation and to have each vote count equally is, it seems to me, basic to the successful operation of a democracy." He called upon the states to take the necessary action to remove voter inequalities:

> I would hope that through the normal political processes, these changes to insure equality of voting and equality of representation would be brought about by the responsible groups involved, in the states and in the national government.

William Beecher in an article in the *Wall Street Journal* entitled "Political Upheaval?" suggested that in the long run the decision could:

Enable metropolitan liberals to wrest control of some state legislative bodies from rural Republicans in the North and West and from conservative Democrats in the South; lead to greater state spending on such urban problems as transportation, schools, slum clearance; bring new prestige, power and patronage to metropolitan machines as they gain strength in state legislatures, and trigger more rapid desegregation efforts in the South as urban leaders gain new leverage vis-à-vis their more tradition-bound rural counterparts.

However, Anthony Lewis, Supreme Court specialist for the New York *Times,* uttered a note of caution. He correctly noted that the actual decision of the Court was quite limited:

. . . [I]n a sense what the Court did not decide was almost as important as what it did. The justices did not say how bad districts would have to be before they would be deemed unconstitutional. In short, they laid down no standards for judging the validity of any particular state's districts. There was a great deal of comment around the country suggesting that the decision would ensure more or less equal population among legislative districts. This is surely a misreading of the opinions.

Moreover, he correctly predicted ". . . it will unquestionably take many years, and many lawsuits, fully to explore the constitutional limits on the drawing of legislative districts."

In New York, Mayor Wagner declared that he was pleased by the Supreme Court decision and that he was directing the city's Corporation Counsel to examine the opinion to determine what further action might be taken on behalf of New York City residents. Moreover, he promised to renew his request that the legislature appoint an impartial group of distinguished citizens to provide for fair and proper apportionment. In Albany, Republican Governor Nelson Rockefeller announced that he had ordered a staff study of legislative reapportionment. However, he took issue with Mayor Wagner's contention that New York City was being discriminated against.

Rockefeller's Republican colleague, Senate Majority Leader Walter J. Mahoney, pledged to fight to bar any change in New York's apportionment formula. "The Supreme Court endorses the method we use in New York now," Senator Mahoney asserted, "and that is the one we are going to use as long as I occupy this chair."

Meanwhile Corporation Counsel Leo A. Larkin said the city would join with radio station WMCA in seeking to overthrow New York State's apportionment formula. Attorneys for WMCA were elated by the Court's decision in the Tennessee apportionment case and the city's subsequent action. As colorfully stated by Leonard Sand: "If a law suit can be compared to horse racing, the *WMCA* case was a bet on a daily double and in *Baker* v. *Carr,* our first entry had carried the field."

The scholarly reaction, as reflected by the numerous articles in the law reviews, was also mixed, but was almost unanimously characterized by a more sophisticated awareness both of what the Court had done and what its decision might entail for politicians and for the judicial system.

One of the harshest criticisms of the Court's decision was an article by Dean Robert Lancaster (College of Arts & Sciences, University of the South) bluntly entitled: "What's Wrong with *Baker* v. *Carr.*" His list of objections contained no fewer than seven major points:

    I. It strikes a crippling blow at our federal system.
   II. It offends democratic theory and practice.
  III. It jeopardizes unnecessarily the judicial function.
  IV. It provides no guide lines for lower court action.
   V. It violates the principle of stare decisis [adherence to judicial precedents] in an artificial and wholly unwarranted manner.
  VI. It is not well reasoned.
 VII. It comes from a fractious and fragmented court.

More temperate in his criticism was Professor Robert G. McCloskey, chairman of the department of government of Harvard University. He recognized that *Baker* v. *Carr* was the most significant decision since *Brown* v. *Board of Education,* the school segregation case of 1954; moreover, he grudgingly conceded that the overwhelmingly favorable response of the general public to the decision might "warrant the conjecture that the Court here happened to hit

upon what the students of public opinion might call a latent consensus. . . . It may be that most Americans have come to think of
some version of the majority principle as at least the presumptive
democratic standard." However, he introduced a note of caution,
warning that: "If the public should ever become convinced that the
Court is merely another legislature, that judicial review is only a
euphemism for an additional layer in the legislative process, the
Court's future as a constitutional tribunal would be cast in grave
doubt."

One of the most favorable responses to *Baker* v. *Carr* was an
article written by Robert B. McKay, associate dean and professor of
law at New York University. Replying specifically to Professor
McCloskey's warning that the public will lose confidence in the Court
if it behaves as a legislature, McKay posed the question: ". . .
[S]hould not the Court equally be concerned about loss of public
confidence for failure to decide where decision *is* called for? Failure
of action where the duty to act is mandatory is at least as grave as a
too-ready willingness to act where artful avoidance is possible." In his
view, the debate as to whether the Court should or should not act
ultimately depends on whether there are judicially manageable standards. For him, the question must be answered in the affirmative:
"Irrational malapportionment of state legislatures does violate the
Fourteenth Amendment; satisfactory judicial standards can be formu-
lated to test the matter; and adequate judicial remedies are available
for correction."

McKay concludes on an optimistic note, emphasizing the positive
aspects of the *Baker* case both for human dignity and for effective
state government:

> *Baker* v. *Carr* marks the full maturation of the libertarian aspects of
> the Equal Protection Clause and provides the courts, federal and
> state alike, with an opportunity to vindicate as a constitutionally
> protected right the assurance to all persons of an opportunity to full
> and equal participation in the principal rite of the democratic process,
> the exercise of the franchise. As state legislatures become more
> fully responsive to the electorate whom they serve there should be
> renewed opportunity for the states to demonstrate the wisdom of re-

serving to the states those powers not committed to the national government. The plea of states' rights can become again the dignified and meaningful claim to separate sovereign rights and obligations that it should always have been, rather than the strident and prideful cry it has sometimes seemed.

4

The Politics
of Apportionment

The Supreme Court's ruling in *Baker* destroyed the rationale of the District Court's decision that it lacked jurisdiction over questions of state apportionment. Consequently, there was little doubt in the minds of any of the attorneys that the *WMCA* case would be remanded for a hearing on its merits. Recognizing this fact, both the appellants and the appellees filed short and perfunctory briefs.

WMCA claimed that the District Court erred in holding that the Fourteenth Amendment did not inhibit the power of a state to discriminate against residents of urban areas. The state replied by arguing that the District Court had in fact considered WMCA's claim on its merits, thus meeting the requirement the Court established in *Baker*.

While WMCA's appeal was pending in the Supreme Court, New York's apportionment was being hotly debated in the political arena. On May 10, 1962, radio station WMCA took the state by surprise by releasing a copy of a previously suppressed report. In 1959, the New York State Commission on the Revision and Simplification of the Constitution, headed by former justice David W. Peck, had commissioned Ruth C. Silva, professor of political science at Pennsylvania State University, to make a study of New York's apportionment. On February 10, 1960, the New York *Times* announced that "the Peck Commission has decided to draft a new legislative apportionment article to the state constitution, over the heated opposition of some Republican legislators and party leaders." However, the Peck Commission Report was never published, at least until it mysteriously came into the hands of R. Peter Straus. Straus revealed to his listeners:

Two years ago the famous Peck Commission received a damning report on how the state cheats New York City out of its fair share of seats in the legislature. That report, by Professor Ruth Silva, was so damning it's never been published.

In fact, out of fear that the Peck Commission might follow up on it, the upstate barons who crack the whip in Albany even went so far as to abolish the commission itself.

Today this very same issue of your right to full representation in the legislature is before the U.S. Supreme Court in a case brought by WMCA.

But meanwhile that report to the Peck Commission remains a state secret. How much longer will the facts be kept from the public?

Well, I'll tell you how long. Until six o'clock tonight. That's when WMCA, having obtained the suppressed report, will make it public. You can hear the facts tonight on WMCA's six o'clock news. They've been swept under the rug long enough.

That same day Straus sent a telegram to Governor Nelson Rockefeller demanding that he summon a special session of the legislature so that it might take "the necessary first steps to amend the constitution to correct the gross inequalities which now make second-class citizens out of urban voters." Four days later, Governor Rockefeller replied. Describing New York's apportionment as "fair," he stated that he saw no reason why he should summon a special session.

The next day (May 15) Mayor Wagner entered the fray. Accusing Rockefeller and the "reactionary" Republican leadership of seeking to "cover up the embezzlement" of a fair share of legislative seats for the majority of New Yorkers living in urban areas, Wagner announced: "The present situation cannot go on much longer. We are making plans. We are preparing to use every proper means to press our demand for equal justice and equal suffrage for New Yorkers in respect to both legislative and Congressional apportionment."

The pressure on the Governor continued to mount and on the morning of June 11, 1962, Rockefeller issued a statement defending his apportionment stand.

EXCERPTS FROM ROCKEFELLER'S STATEMENT

In assessing the basic "fairness" of the present New York apportionment formula, I find that certain considerations are often overlooked.

Some, for example, claim that the New York Legislature is dominated by "rural interests" although it is a fact that now, as in the case of each apportionment under the 1894 formula, the ten most populous urban and suburban counties in the state have a clear majority in legislative strength—in both houses.

Some have claimed that the application of the 1894 formula requires increasing under-representation of the state's urban and suburban areas with each successive apportionment. Yet:

In 1943, the ten most populous counties represented 73.1 per cent of the state's 1940 population and were allocated ninety-three of the 150 seats in the Assembly and thirty-six of the fifty-six Senate seats.

In 1953, the ten most populous counties (then as now the counties of Kings, Queens, New York, Bronx, Nassau, Erie, Westchester, Suffolk, Monroe and Onondaga) represented 73.6 per cent of the state's 1950 population and were allocated the same number of Assembly seats—ninety-three—and thirty-eight of the fifty-eight Senate seats, and

A further apportionment under the 1894 formula based on the 1960 census figures would allocate Assembly and Senate seats in accordance with population movements since 1950, but the legislative strength of the ten most populous counties, which represent 73.5 per cent of the state's 1960 population, would remain the same in the Assembly and virtually the same in the Senate.

*   *   *

Those who find "unfairness" in the constitutional guarantee of one Assembly seat for each county, or in the Senate districting requirement which prevents a county from being subdivided except to form a complete Senate district, tend to assume that the only test of "fairness" is equality in the number of citizens living in each legislative district. If this position is accepted for the state of New York, is it somehow less unfair:

That in the United States Senate, Senator [Jacob] Javits and Senator [Kenneth] Keating represent 16,782,304 while the two Senators from Alaska represent only 226,167?

That in the United States Senate, the Senators from the nine states with a majority of the nation's population have only eighteen of the 100 Senators?

That in the United States House of Representatives, the State of Alaska is assured one Congressman for its 226,167 people and the state of New Hampshire, two Congressmen, each representing an average of 303,460 people, while in the State of New York each Congressman represents an average of 409,326?

That the least populous Congressional district in the state of Arizona —a state with 1,302,161 people—should have only 198,000 people while the least populous New York Congressional district has 348,940 people?

That on the Board of Estimate of the City of New York, the Borough of Richmond has two votes for its 221,991 people while the Borough of Brooklyn has the same number of votes for its 2,627,319 people?

Furthermore, to apportion each Assembly seat and each State Senate seat solely on the basis of the population would make county lines irrelevant both in apportioning the number of the seats and in drawing district lines.

My purpose in raising these matters is to indicate the difficulties of basing standards of "fairness" for apportionment purposes strictly and solely on equality of population when many other factors, such as traditions of local government, the economic and social patterns of local areas, increasing responsibilities for local governments, population movements and the effectiveness of legislative representation when districts cover an unusually large geographic area, must all be considered.

In light of these difficulties and because I believe that the atmosphere of an election year campaign is not conducive to a dispassionate reappraisal of the existing formula, I have determined not to convene the legislature in special session at this time to consider possible amendments of the existing New York apportionment formula.

The Governor's timing was unfortunate. The same day Rockefeller released his statement, the Supreme Court, in a brief per curium opinion, vacated the three-judge court's decision in the *WMCA* case and remanded it to the lower court for a hearing on its merits in light of the Court's decision in *Baker* v. *Carr*. Justice Harlan dissented from the Court's order, arguing that the appeal should be dismissed for want of a substantial federal question or, failing that, the Court itself should consider "whether the Equal Protection Clause of the Fourteenth Amendment is violated by a state apportionment of seats in both its legislative chambers on other than a substantially proportional populative basis."

If the Supreme Court's action gladdened the heart of WMCA's R. Peter Straus, it certainly didn't make life easier for New York's Governor Rockefeller. On June 12, 1962, J. Lee Rankin, United States Solicitor General during the Eisenhower administration, sent the Governor the following telegram:

June 12, 1962

The Honorable Nelson A. Rockefeller
The Governor of the State of New York
Albany, New York

Yesterday's decision of the U.S. Supreme Court, remanding the WMCA challenge to the constitutionality of the state apportionment for a full trial on the merits, raises profound questions as to the proper action which a governor of a state should take while such a suit is pending. Specifically in New York, the question is whether you as Governor should call a special session of the legislature. My opinion is that you should for several reasons.

.   .   .

I sense that there is some confusion as to the appropriate role of the courts and the legislature in this area of the law for you are quoted as saying that you would take no action on the matter while it is "before the courts." While such an attitude of abstention pending judicial action is quite appropriate with regard to most litigation, a clearly manifested desire of the Supreme Court is precisely that the legislatures would act so that the actual reapportionment of the state would not come as a result of judicial fiat but from the elected representatives of the people. Indeed, the *WMCA* complaint specifically contemplates such action for it does not ask the court to reapportion but rather to assume and retain jurisdiction while the legislature itself acts on the problem. . . .

I know that it was the sincere hope of the United States Department of Justice at the time the decision was made to intervene as amicus curiae in *Baker* v. *Carr* that, following Supreme Court action, the state governments would seize the initiative in bringing about a reformation. . . . The fact that the decision to lend federal support to the plaintiffs in the *Baker* case was made under the Republican administration is a fact you will not want to overlook today. Reapportionment need not and should not be a partisan political issue. . . .

Further, the mechanisms and timetables of the amendatory process make it imperative that you act promptly on this issue. Since a constitutional amendment must be approved by two separately elected legislatures before submission to popular referendum, a special session of the legislature would enable constitutional revision—apart from court action—by 1964. If no action is taken before January 1963, a two-year delay results during which time the inequities continue.

I suggest, therefore, that you should reconsider calling a special session of the legislature in the light of yesterday's ruling by the Supreme Court on the *WMCA* case. . . . What is required is that prompt legislative consideration be given to a decision as to which of the various corrective proposals suggested in that report best suit the needs of this state.

As the Republican Governor of New York, you alone have the power and the opportunity to take the leadership on this issue.

J. Lee Rankin

The Governor's persistent refusal to call a special legislative session also met with disfavor in the press. In an article in the New York *Herald-Tribune,* Laurence Barrett concluded that no matter what action Rockefeller took on apportionment he stood to loose ground politically.

Mr. Rockefeller could reverse his stand and call an immediate special session of the legislature to begin work on changing the constitutional formula. This is highly unlikely. If it happened, the Democrats could justly take credit for forcing reform and the Governor's own party would be furious with him.

The special three-man federal court soon to review a citizen's suit at the direction of the United States Supreme Court could order a drastic revision. At this late stage in an election year political chaos would result. Again, the Democrats would have a good issue and the Governor would get the blame because he did not take the initiative early enough to avoid confusion.

The court action could bog down, leaving the legislative lines unchanged for this year. While this would deprive the Democrats of a chance for majorities in both houses of the legislature, it would give them an excellent talking point in the state-wide contests.

The liberal New York *Post* took advantage of Rockefeller's vulnerable position and denounced him in a vehement editorial. Replying to Rockefeller's statement that an election year was not conducive to "a dispassionate" reappraisal of the formula, the *Post* asked:

> But what better year is there than an election year to have the legislature consider revision of a formula which affects every voter in the state? Revision during an election year would give the electorate a chance to pass judgment on the handiwork of the Governor and his aides. Presumably that is what they fear.

Democratic state officials leaped at the opportunity to spike Rockefeller's presidential ambitions. William K. McKeon, Democratic state chairman, said that the Governor "wouldn't dare change the unfair formula which guarantees Republican control of the legislature." He pictured the Governor as "walking a tightrope between fair-minded persons and old-line Republican diehards." Nassau County Executive Eugene Nickerson commented that Rockefeller's position "would compel us to pin all our hopes for relief on the federal courts. It displays not only a distressing lack of leadership but also a curious departure from "do-it-yourself" home rule—a principle that his party seems to honor more in the breach than in the observance."

Rockefeller, however, was not entirely without political support. Assembly Speaker Joseph F. Carlino stated that he did not expect the federal courts to find the legislative districting in New York State so far out of line that it violates the equal protection guarantees of the United States Constitution. But if they do, he added, "they'll be usurping for the first time in the history of the United States what has generally been conceded to be a legislative prerogative of the respective state governments."

5

A Trial on the Merits

Judges Levet, Ryan and Waterman set August 1, 1962 as the date for hearing WMCA's case. Leonard Sand, in a brief filed with the special three-man court, urged a speedy disposition of the case. Noting that WMCA's complaint had been filed over thirteen months before "with the avowed purpose of procuring relief prior to the November, 1962 elections," Sand pointed out that there was still time, if the Court took swift action, to grant the desired relief. If the Court were to rule New York's apportionment provisions invalid, the legislature could immediately enact a statute to govern the next election. Moreover, if the legislature did not take action, three possible courses of action would nevertheless be available: (1) the Court could itself fashion a reapportionment, possibly through a special master; (2) the Court could order an election at large; and (3) the Court could decree that the election be held in existing districts but that the vote of each member of the legislature be weighted on the basis of 1960 population in the respective districts.

On the substantive issue of whether New York's apportionment was constitutional, Sand argued that invidious geographical discrimination violates the Fourteenth Amendment, that such malapportionment did in fact exist and that the burden of proof therefore shifted to the defendant, New York State, who must demonstrate that the apportionment was rational. In support of his brief, Sand appended affidavits from Professor Ruth C. Silva and R. Peter Straus. Professor Silva documented with statistics the population disparities characterizing New York's urban and rural Assembly and Senate districts Straus sought to demonstrate that, as a result of malapportionment, New York City residents were suffering economic discrimination.

In a reply brief, Attorney General Louis J. Lefkowitz asked for

the dismissal of WMCA's suit, stating that the imminence of the
1962 legislative elections made it impractical for the Court to grant
the demanded relief:

> Pursuant to the New York State Election Law, primary elections are
> to be held on September 5, 1962; designating petitions are now being
> circulated and must be filed between July 31 and August 7, 1962; and
> independent nominating petitions must be filed during the week be-
> ginning September 17, 1962. Thus, the granting of an injunction would
> in effect prevent the election of a new legislature, contrary to the best
> interests of the people of the State of New York.

In addition to this argument, Lefkowitz offered several major
points of defense: (1) the Court lacked jurisdiction over apportionment cases; (2) judicial remedies were lacking; (3) the people were
not without means of changing New York's apportionment provisions
since they possessed the right to convene a constitutional convention
without the approval of the legislature; (4) the voters repeatedly refused to alter the formula for apportioning members of the legislature;
and (5) the apportionment provisions did not violate the Fourteenth
Amendment.

Hearings began on Wednesday morning, August 1, and WMCA
immediately ran into trouble. The Court refused to consider two
major points pressed by WMCA and New York City: that the legislature, in devising the apportionment formula in 1894, had done so
with the deliberate intent to deny urban centers adequate representation, and that the city had been cheated of millions of dollars in state
financial aid as a result of the rural dominance of the two houses of
the legislature.

After preliminary skirmishing over the admissibility of evidence and
testimony of witnesses (the Court decided to consider only factual
evidence excluding expert commentary and arguments), the discussion swiftly moved to the heart of the issue: the criteria on which
apportionments might legitimately be based.

EXCERPTS FROM THE TRANSCRIPT

Mr. Sand: We start with a base for measuring an apportionment
with people, because government above all else represents people. . . .

[N]o matter what the talk may be of interests or local subdivisions, what we are talking about is to what extent the people of the state will be represented in their legislature, and we respectfully submit to this Court that any system of apportionment which gives greater weight to the votes of citizens because they reside in one area of the state than it does to the votes of other citizens residing elsewhere contains within it an implict value judgment that some citizens of the state are worthier of representation, having a right to the disproportionate say in the government than other people.

We respectfully submit that such a value judgment implemented by state action as it is in New York is contrary to the Equal Protection Clause of the Fourteenth Amendment.

Thomas Jefferson said: "Equal representation is so fundamental a principle in a true republic that no prejudices can justify its violation because the prejudices themselves cannot be justified."

The issue is not whether all the people of the state are to be represented but whether some people are to be represented disproportionately to their numbers, and who is to say which people and on what basis they are to be preferred.

These are value judgments which the Equal Protection Clause does not permit. There cannot be some citizens more equal than others under the Fourteenth Amendment.

• • •

Judge Ryan: Is it your position that substantial equality is a constitutional requirement?

Mr. Sand: It is my position that the Fourteenth Amendment requires that the apportionment of the state legislature be proportionate to population and that there must be a direct and approximate relationship between the population of the state and the apportionment of the Legislature.

• • •

Judge Ryan: Don't you lose sight of the fact that our representatives are chosen not as representatives of an urban or of a rural district, but rather as representatives of one of the two major political parties, and that we hear . . . of representatives of both major parties coming from districts within an urban area?

Mr. Sand: I recognize the party system in New York State.

Judge Ryan: Isn't that the system by which legislation is enacted
. . . rather than by a system of choosing representatives—

Mr. Sand: I respectfully call your Honor's attention to the fact that
in New York State by virtue of the malapportionment, the party which
receives the majority of the votes does not elect the majority of the
state legislature, so that in New York State malapportionment brings
it about that the people having a party preference in the majority are
unable to implement that preference, and in this respect New York
is probably the worst malapportioned state in the nation. . . .

Judge Ryan: Would you recognize that there is no longer a population with any real permanency which can be described as urban
population, and that there is a constant flux and movement, not only
within the state but throughout the nation, of people who formerly lived
in the city and moved out to rural areas?

Mr. Sand: I recognize it, your Honor, and rely on it, because I
think that the mobility of the population indicates the arbitrariness,
the irrationality in saying that where a particular citizen happens to be
at a particular time is determinative of how much weight should be
given to his vote in the legislature.

I think that what your Honor has pointed out is that notions of
localism, of the significance of the political subdivisions, which developed at an earlier time in the history of the state, and at a time
when there was a more uniform population dispersal throughout the
state, are now anachronistic and obsolete and are preserved solely
for the purpose of perpetuating a system which is discriminatory
towards the persons in the class of the plaintiffs.

.   .   .

Judge Levet: Do you think that there is anything inherently unconstitutional in each county having an Assemblyman? In other words,
do you contend that there should be no geographic weight whatsoever?

.   .   .

Mr. Sand: I say, yes, it is permissible to have one representative
per county if the overall consequence of the apportionment system is
not to arrive at a legislature in neither house of which is there proportionate representation of population.

Judge Waterman: Let me ask you a question. There is an area in
the State of New York which is particularly bad from your point
of view, because there are very few people in it . . . because it repre-

sents a natural vacational ground, the preservation of natural resources and the like. Should it have an equal representation or should it not?

Mr. Sand: It should have representation. But the fact that the people—

Judge Waterman: Is it of interest to the people of the State of New York to have their vacational areas protected?

Mr. Sand: Of course it is of interest to the people who reside there and those who vacation there. That is why I emphasize that the contention which is being made is not that there should be any area of the state or any interest of the state which is not represented, but if you say that because the people who vote in that area reside in that area, their vote is of greater significance than those who reside elsewhere, you are saying that because they vote there they are worthier of representation, they are somehow better.

.   .   .

We submit to this Court, we have shown or attempted to show by the only means by which it is possible to show that the apportionment of this state is based upon a judgment which prefers one group of citizens to another in violation of the Equal Protection Clause, and that therefore the apportionment of this state is not in conformity with the Fourteenth Amendment.

After Sand concluded his argument, the Court took a short recess. Upon reconvening, the justices began to interrogate attorneys for other parties to the suit. Eugene Nickerson, Nassau County Executive, took advantage of this opportunity to point out the discrimination in representation that Nassau County voters faced.

Mr. Nickerson: . . . I would like to point out the significance of this case to Nassau County. Since the 1950 census, we have doubled in size. We had three State Senators, as we now do as a result of the 1950 census, the apportionment under that census. Under the new apportionment we will still have three State Senators so that although we have doubled in size, from 650,000 persons to almost 1,300,000, we will still have the same number of Senators.

Monroe County, which will have less than half of our population, will have the same number of Senators as we do.

Now, in the Senate, on the average our senatorial districts are two and a half times as large as the smaller Senate districts. In the Assembly . . . we are outweighted by about five to one.

Schuyler County . . . had an Assemblyman for less than 15,000 population. Our largest Assembly district has 340,000. So it means that it requires approximately twenty-three votes in Nassau County to [equal] one vote in Schuyler County.

The Court, having heard the testimony and arguments of those seeking to overturn New York's apportionment, next turned to the main defendant: New York State. Irving Galt, assistant solicitor general sought to rebut WMCA's contentions by arguing that the state's apportionment met the rationality test imposed by the Fourteenth Amendment.

Mr. Galt: I think one could not have listened to the plaintiff's counsel arguing this case without realizing, to begin with, that the entire argument is predicated on the notion that there must be constitutionally an arithmetical basis for the representation of a state legislature, and, first of all, I want to say that this is not what *Baker* v. *Carr* held. . . . [The test] is . . . what is equal and what is equal protection in the eyes of the law and how best a legislature may represent . . . the people, and that does not mean simply representing them on a strict or as close to a strict numerical basis as possible. The *MacDougall* case [*MacDougall* v. *Green*] is still law . . . and [it] of course holds that the function of government is [not] simply to represent numbers [but also] to take into account, among other things, such elements as the diffusion of population, the interests of the thinly-populated counties. This is a composite of interests which must be taken into account.

Let us, for example, take one of the several elements. There are elements other than population. There is such a thing as community of interest which the counties to such a great extent and so very well exemplify. There are such things as geographical considerations, and there are other considerations which may very properly belong within a consistent, reasonable, rational apportionment system, such as New York's undoubtedly is.

Now, let us take geography alone for a moment. . . . The Assemblyman, for instance, from St. Lawrence County—I guess that is the northeast corner of the State—represents an area covering no less than 2,767 square miles. Now, that is larger than the State of

Delaware. Just to mention 2,700 miles in a moment may not give us the full conception, but here is one county of the state actually larger than the State of Delaware, and I believe it is by no means the largest county.

He represents very few people, comparatively. The plaintiffs say comparatively few people. But that constituency is spread over an extremely large geographical area.

. . .

Now much was suggested by Mr. Sand on the very interesting and intriguing subject of bicameralism. I confess that for the life of me I cannot follow an argument such as was made here; that it is all right for one house to be geared to population only and all right for another house to be geared to something else, which immediately opens the door to considering other factors, and then by a neat little argumentative arrangement, by a little adroit presentation, suggesting what on its face sounds seemingly reasonable and plausible, that is very nice to have one house one way and one the other; but one of the many difficulties with this interesting little theory, as I see it, is that the greatest model for the theory of bicameralism—our own United States legislature, the House of Representatives and Congress—I think it is beyond peradventure of doubt that neither the House nor the Senate is on a strictly population basis. The Senate beyond argument and the states themselves use the very same basis that we use: have representation, regardless of population, for every single state in the United States.

Doesn't that belie the entire theory and claim of the plaintiffs? . . . If indeed the suggestion Mr. Sand offers does not actually violate the federal model, and if it is rational to represent population only in one house and other factors only in the second, what is irrational, what is wrong, what is unreasonable, what is invidiously discriminatory about having a composite of those same factors in both houses?

The Court handed down its decision on August 16, 1962: WMCA's complaint was dismissed on its merits. Judge Levet again wrote the Court's opinion. He enumerated five "tests" to determine an apportionment's constitutionality: (1) whether the system is arbitrary; (2) whether the allocation of seats has an historical basis; (3) whether a political remedy exists; (4) geography and the accessibility of legislators to their constituency; and (5) whether the Court would have to invalidate provisions in the state constitution. New York's system passed all these tests.

Levet, reviewing the Assembly provisions, found that "the net result is that Assemblymen (subject to the minimum provision per county, like the minimum provision for members in the federal House of Representatives) are in fact substantially based on citizen population." Nor were the Senate provisions deemed irrational or arbitrary. They were "designed to effectuate administration of the senatorial electorate, and designed to meet accessibility, and practicability."

The Court thus concluded, after considering each of the five tests, that: "The apportionment provisions of the State of New York are rational, not arbitrary, are of substantially historical origin, contain no geographical discrimination, permit an electoral majority to alter or change the same and are not unconstitutional under the relevant decisions of the United States Supreme Court."

Judge Ryan, who filed a concurring opinion, emphasized two points: that political remedies (constitutional convention) were available; and that New York's apportionment represented a rational attempt to prevent undue concentration of political power. He noted that:

The six plaintiff counties contain 56.2% of the state's population, but they contain only 3.1% of its area. If apportionment were based solely on population, this would mean that 3% of the state's area would dominate the rest of New York. Even if the urban representatives were to sincerely endeavor to care for the interests of the state as a whole, it is unlikely that they might be able to fully understand the problems of the remaining vast area of the state. Each rural member of the legislature presently represents a much greater area than his urban counterpart. If population were to be made the sole criterion of apportionment, the area per representative in certain districts would increase even further. Representatives might not adequately represent localities which were not their home and, correspondingly, the residents of these localities might lose the benefits of the democratic governmental process.

6

Before the High Court

"The ruling [of the District Court in the *WMCA* case] was a major victory for Governor Rockefeller and the leaders of the Republican controlled legislature," reported the New York *Times*.

> They had insisted that the apportionment formula, as applied by the legislature, was fair to all sections. . . .
> The ruling struck a blow at the hopes of Mayor Wagner and other leading Democrats to use the "discrimination" issue as a major weapon. . . .

Straus, although chagrined, was not disheartened. He encouraged his listeners:

> WMCA's lawyers advise us that we have strong grounds for another appeal to the Supreme Court. WMCA will make that appeal. We are in this battle to the end—a battle to make you a first-class citizen of New York State.

On August 29, 1962, WMCA did in fact appeal the District Court's ruling to the Supreme Court. In a jurisdictional statement filed to persuade the Court to grant a review to WMCA's suit, the radio station's attorneys argued that the District Court had erred both in excluding evidence and in formulating a test for apportionments. The lower court, they noted, had rejected their offers to prove that:

> a) the apportionment formula was specifically designed and intended to curtail the representation of urban residents;
> b) the malapportioned legislature in fact discriminated against urban residents in allocating tax revenues and distributing benefits;

    c) that a consensus of expert opinion deemed relationship to population to be the only fair and equitable basis to measure the validity of an apportionment system.

    Leo Larkin, corporation counsel of the City of New York, filed a brief in behalf of Paul Screvane, president of the City Council, and other city officials, supporting radio station WMCA in its attempt to upset New York's apportionment. In addition to citing statistics meant to demonstrate voting inequities, Larkin also considered the substantive question of what standards state apportionment must meet. Whereas WMCA merely asked the Court to rule that at least one house must be apportioned strictly on the basis of population, the city took the position that "the only valid method of apportionment under the Equal Protection Clause is for both houses of the legislature to be proportionate to population."

    In marked contrast, Louis Lefkowitz, attorney general of the State of New York moved "that the final judgment of the District Court be affirmed on the ground that the question [whether the Fourteenth Amendment's Equal Protection Clause required state legislatures to apportion at least one house on a population basis] is so unsubstantial as not to warrant further argument, or, in the alternative, that the appeal be dismissed."

    While the litigants were awaiting disposition of WMCA's appeal, the Supreme Court took action in a related field. On March 18, 1963, by an 8-1 vote, it held in *Gray* v. *Sanders* that Georgia's county unit system of weighting votes in state-wide elections violated the Equal Protection Clause of the Fourteenth Amendment. There was considerable uncertainty as to what the effect of *Gray* would be in state apportionment cases. The specific holding of the case was limited to equality of voting power within a single constituency. If strictly applied, *Gray* would mean only that the vote of each citizen within a *legislative district* must have equal value. On the other hand, Justice Douglas had spoken in broad terms of the fundamental principle of "one man, one vote," and had denounced the idea that a state could set up a "preferred class" of voters. Could such broad statements be limited to the specific situation in Georgia? Was there any rational justification for not extending them to apportionments? The logic of the decision *could* be extended to the *WMCA* case: It was arguable that, because a legislature can affect every citizen, the Equal Protection Clause guaranteed equal value in legislative elections to every citizen's vote.

On June 10, 1963, the Supreme Court noted probable jurisdiction of WMCA's appeal. In a colorful broadcast, R. Peter Straus, both applauded the Court's decision and urged Governor Rockefeller to take action to correct New York's discriminatory apportionment.

> WMCA and the voters of New York State are cheering today's call by the nation's chief umpire. In deciding to hear WMCA's case, the Supreme Court has given New Yorkers up and down the state another turn at bat. We may be home soon.
>
> Nelson Rockefeller, unfortunately, has yet to take his cuts against the unfair apportionment of New York's state legislature. Earlier this year, when one bill for apportionment reform was killed in committee, the citizens of his state heard not one word of complaint from Nelson Rockefeller. The Governor seems to prefer the security of the dugout to real action against New York's legislative malapportionment.

Pressure on the Governor also came from the daily press. A New York *Times* editorial sedately reminded readers that:

> The Court's newly adopted role as overseer in this field [legislative apportionment] does not, of course, alter the primary responsibility of the states themselves to correct manifest inequities in legislative and congressional districting. Under the rules now in effect here, one vote for Assemblyman in Schuyler County has the same weight as fourteen in Suffolk and one vote for State Senator in Monroe is equal to two in Manhattan. Whether or not the Supreme Court holds this imbalance sufficient to violate equal protection under the federal Constitution, New York's nineteenth-century formula is overdue for revision by the legislature. Governor Rockefeller ought not to wait for the Court to order a change; a non-partisan commission could begin right away to draft recommendations for a fairer plan.

Even rural politicians favored action. Senator Robert C. McEwen of Ogdensburg, chairman of the Joint Legislative Committee on Reapportionment, declared that he was "absolutely" in favor of a special session late in November. Reflecting that he didn't "think that the Governor has been thoroughly advised of the time factors involved," McEwen stated that population changes since the last reapportionment in 1953 had made it obligatory for the legislature to act promptly. Governor Rockefeller, however, remained impervious to criticism. He maintained that New York's apportionment was fair and, in any event, should not be changed while litigation was pending in the Supreme Court.

In order to present the strongest possible legal case, Sand wished to coordinate the approaches of WMCA with its allies. His attempt, however, proved unsuccessful. As recalled by Jack B. Weinstein, professor of law at Columbia University and Nassau County attorney, "the attorneys for Nassau and New York City met with Sand in the summer of 1963. There was a possibility of filing a joint brief but we decided against it because it would be unseemly for private individuals and municipal entities to join together against the state. Besides, Nassau had a very appealing case."

While the lawyers worked on their briefs, radio station WMCA issued a steady stream of editorials criticizing all who opposed its reapportionment drive. Typical of this propaganda barrage was a broadcast of August 4, 1963:

> In our State Assembly, Paul Taylor of Yates County represents barely a tenth as many voters as the average Assemblyman from New York City.
>
> That's exactly why WMCA has asked the U.S. Supreme Court to rule that the apportionment of our legislature violates your constitutional rights.
>
> But upstate Assemblyman Taylor disagrees. "Civic virtue," he says, "lives in the country." By contrast, he implies, the big city breeds all kinds of Communists, killers and nuts.
>
> Now the notion of virtue as a qualification for voting is interesting in a way. But it might be hard to prove that a roadside bookie in Yates County is ten times as virtuous as, say, Cardinal Spellman.
>
> And it might be hard to explain why the legislative spokesman for

our virtuous yeoman upstate make an annual practice of stealing New York City blind when it comes to voting state aid.

If that's civic virtue, WMCA takes a stand for sin.

In September, 1963, WMCA, New York City and Nassau County filed their briefs with the Supreme Court. Although they had been prepared separately, they agreed in the major particulars. All three asserted that population was the only constitutional standard by which to apportion. All three pointed to the arbitrary character of New York's system of apportionment. There were, however, significant differences in emphasis.

An idea of the scope of a brief filed in the Supreme Court can first be gleaned by noting the major entries in the Index of WMCA's brief.

INDEX

Opinions Below

Jurisdiction

United States Constitution, Federal Statutes and State Constitution and Statutes Involved

Questions Presented

Statements

    A) The Complaint

    B) The Prior Proceedings

    C) The Opinions Below

Summary of Argument

Argument

    I. The Apportionment of the New York State Legislature; the Causes and Extent of Malapportionment in Both Houses of the Legislature.

        a. The History of Apportionment in New York Prior to 1894

        b. The Present Method of Legislative Apportionment

            (i) Introduction

            (ii) The Senate Apportionment Formula

            (iii) The Assembly Apportionment Formula

        c. The Nature and Extent of Malapportionment

            (i) Geographical Discrimination

(ii) Irrational "Horizontal" Disparities—The New York Crazy Quilt

II. The Provisions Governing the Apportionment of the New York State Legislature Are Violative of the Fourteenth Amendment

a. In General

b. *MacDougall* v. *Green* and *Gray* v. *Sanders*

c. Apportionment Must Be Proportionate to Population

d. The Constitutional Provisions for Apportionment of Both Houses of the Legislature Should Be Invalidated

III. The District Court Did Not Rehear and Reconsider in the Manner Contemplated by this Court's Remand

a. The District Court erred in placing an undue burden of proof on appellants

b. The District Court erred in refusing to consider the purpose and intent of the apportionment provisions and the economic consequences of malapportionment

(i) Purpose and intent

(ii) Economic consequences of malapportionment; deprivation of due process

IV. Appellants Lack Any Practical Political Remedy; the Need for Judicial Intervention is as Great Here as in *Baker* v. *Carr* and *Gray* v. *Sanders*

Conclusions

Appendix A (Statutes)

Appendix B (Historical Summary of Prior Apportionment Provisions)

Appendix C (The Constitutional Convention of 1894)

The three basic contentions of Sand and Gross were that: New York's apportionment provisions necessarily result in great and arbitrary disproportions between population and representation in both houses of the legislature and systematically discriminate against residents of the most heavily populated areas of the state; the apportionment formula was adopted with a deliberate purpose and intent to limit the representation of residents of the most heavily populated areas of the state; and that as a result of this malapportionment, urban residents are victims of economic discrimination and are deprived of due process of law.

The constitutional issue Sand and Gross raised was: What limits does the Equal Protection Clause set upon state apportionments? The Fourteenth Amendment prohibits "invidious discriminations." The question to be considered is: What constitutes improper discrimination?

The brief filed by Leo Larkin, city corporation counsel, agreed in the main with WMCA's; its major contribution, however, was its wealth of statistical evidence, some thirty pages in all. Among the statistics offered in his brief was evidence supporting his argument that New York's apportionment provisions favored the Republican party:

	Election	Vote for Democratic Candidates	Vote for Republican Candidates	Democrats Elected	Republicans Elected
	1958	2,735,360	2,712,456	58	92
Assembly:	1960	3,557,043	3,309,830	66	84
	1962	2,703,686	2,681,452	65	85
	1958	2,732,471	2,703,309	24	34
Senate:	1960	3,525,787	3,277,503	25	33
	1962	2,714,107	2,709,435	25	33

Nassau County Attorney Jack B. Weinstein presented a concrete picture of the discrimination faced by growing suburbia. He pointed out, as County Executive Eugene Nickerson had in the District Court, that "despite the fact that Nassau's population increased from 655,690 in 1950 to 1,275,801 in 1960—an increase which almost doubled it —Nassau County will not obtain a single additional Senator upon reapportionment. This anomaly results from the fact that previously Nassau had less than 6% of the population while now it has more than 6% of the state's population, and counties falling into the latter category are specifically discriminated against by the apportionment scheme."

To prove that Nassau's residents were not "inferior" to upstate rural inhabitants, Weinstein presented charts that showed conclusively that Nassau's citizens were better educated, were employed in superior occupations, and had higher incomes than their rural counterparts. However, their vote as shown was considerably less valuable:

	Voting Power Ratio Based upon Present Apportionment		Voting Power Ratio Based upon Prospective Apportionment	
	Assembly	Senate	Assembly	Senate
Nassau				
(average district)	1	1	1	1
Essex	6.1	2.6	3.7	2.6
Warren	4.9	2.6	2.9	2.6
Saratoga	2.4	2.6	1.5	2.6
Schuyler	14.3	2.1	8.6	2.1

WMCA was also joined in its litigation efforts by three groups noted for their dedication to protecting the rights of the individual: The American Civil Liberties Union, the American Jewish Congress, and the Legal Defense and Educational Fund of the National Association for the Advancement of Colored People. Their appearance as amici curiae was enthusiastically noted by R. Peter Straus. In a broadcast on September 9, 1963, he exclaimed:

> Today's action by three great citizens' groups put WMCA among the best company in the nation. Equal rights for all the citizens of New York State—rural, urban and suburban: This is the real meaning WMCA sees in the brief for apportionment reform filed today by the American Jewish Congress, the American Civil Liberties Union, and the Legal Defense Fund of the National Association for the Advancement of Colored People.
>
> True democracy means equal rights for voters regardless of address —just as it means equal protection of the laws regardless of race, color or creed.

The special role of an amicus curiae is to bring to the attention of the Court essentially non-legal material which it might otherwise inadvertently overlook. Emphasis is generally placed on the broad social policies which underlie the issues raised in the litigation. The joint brief filed by Dean Robert B. McKay of the New York University School of Law on behalf of the three organizations admirably performed this important function. McKay began by informing the Court of the effect of malapportionment upon the classes of citizens represented by his clients:

> Each of the amici has a special interest in assuring equal recognition for the social, economic, and political interests of minority groups that have been particular targets of majority discrimination, whether on grounds of race, religion, national origin, or because of the expression of unpopular political beliefs. These minority groups tend to concentrate in the most populous areas, perhaps because they find there greater numbers with like interests, possibly because they can in the cities achieve greater anonymity, or simply because the cities have ordinarily given more hospitable shelter to minority interest groups. . . . The amici are accordingly especially sensitive to discrimination against the urban voter because of the resulting partial disfranchisement of minority groups.

McKay's major contribution was his perceptive analysis of the arguments advanced in favor of apportionment on a non-population basis. He considered in turn five factors: area, history, federal analogy, availability of the initiative, and governmental boundaries.

EXCERPTS FROM MCKAY'S BRIEF

A. *Area*

The claim that special weight should be given to geography is self-refuting. Pastures, rivers and trees do not vote and do not deserve representation in state legislatures. Government does not exist for their benefit. No one suggests that legislators should be chosen from uninhabited areas.

• • •

B. *History*

The appeal to history in justification for inequalities of voter representation cannot withstand analysis under the challenge of the Equal Protection Clause of the Fourteenth Amendment, which must be read in the present tense. If a given apportionment plan produces gross inequality, it cannot be saved by showing either that the inequality has *existed or that it developed gradually over a long period of time. Institutions are justified by history only if it shows that they have worked well. Moreover . . . departures from equality of representation can be justified, if at all, only by the need to serve compelling public objectives. Preservation of long-continued practice is not such an objective.**

•   •   •

Departures from the salutary principle did not become widespread until the latter part of the nineteenth century. Although the original constitutions of thirty-six states required that representation be based completely, or almost so, on population, subsequently "this pattern was to change because of the growth of big cities." The further distortions of the twentieth century are notorious, further aggravated by the sharp acceleration of the population shift, first to the cities and then to the suburbs, and the frequent legislative failure to act in compliance with state constitutional commands for reapportionment. No theory of constitutional law justifies using this recent history to sanction ever widening departures from the principle of equality.

C. *The Federal Analogy*

A variant of the historical argument is the claim that population can be altogether disregarded in one, if not both, houses of a bicameral legislature because that is the pattern adopted in the federal Congress. . . .

. . . We submit that the federal analogy should be rejected, and equal representation be required in both houses, for several independent reasons.

1. The Constitution itself rejects the relevance of analogies drawn to the method of selection of members of the two houses of Congress. The allotment of two Senators to each state is made not by legislative act but by an express constitutional provision which was the result of a necessary political compromise. . . .

2. The truth is that reliance on the federal analogy seems to be principally an after-the-fact rationalization in support of a variety of legislative apportionment schemes, many of which have very little in common with the congressional plan of representation. . . .

•   •   •

*Author's italics.

3. Counties and towns, unlike states, have no sovereign existence apart from the state which created them and which could at any time alter their boundaries or terminate their existence. The national government was founded by the states and was thus their creature, but the relationship between the states and their political subdivisions is exactly opposite. States are guaranteed against dismemberment without their consent and the Tenth Amendment guarantees to the several states all powers not delegated to the federal government or specifically forbidden in the Constitution. No such provisions protect towns or counties from the plenary powers of the states over their existence, functioning, and representation in the legislature.

. . .

4. It is argued that accommodation to full equality of voter representation in both houses of a state legislature would destroy the purpose of the bicameral legislative body. But this is largely based upon an appeal to what is constitutionally irrelevant and factually erroneous. There is nothing inherently sacred in the bicameral concept.

It is not, however, necessary to reject the strong American tradition in favor of bicameralism. Even when full equality of election districts is achieved in both houses of a state legislature, each house can continue to serve a separate and distinct function. In nearly every state, the terms of office are different in the two houses so that members of one house seek renewal of their elective mandate more frequently than in the other. Moreover, the constituencies are ordinarily different. In a typical situation, each member of the upper house has two to four times as many constituents in his district as does his lower house colleague. As a result the member of the lower house ordinarily has a more homogeneous constituency whose views he can represent with parochial narrowness while his counterpart in the other chamber must necessarily accommodate himself to a greater variety of views.

5. *The most important reason of all for rejecting the federal analogy derives directly from the democratic principle. There is no justification for allowing any minority interest group, whether rural voters or any other, to gain absolute control of a state legislature with concomitant power to enact legislation which is unacceptable to the majority. It is one thing to preserve restraint upon majority action through the power of executive veto, by special majorities for change of organic law, by bills of rights, and otherwise. But it is quite an-*

*other matter, and utterly indefensible, to place in the hands of a
minority the power to enact positive legislation along with the power
to prevent diminution of its own dominant role in the legislative
process.*

•   •   •

*It remains only for this Court to state unequivocally the primacy
of the equal-population principle, leaving implementation to state
legislatures. Ordinarily, no more drastic remedy will be necessary than
a clear statement as to the requirements of equal protection in the
context of apportionment and districting, while directing the appropriate lower federal courts and state courts to retain jurisdiction pending
prompt and complete legislative correction. The sanction of more
drastic judicial action should thus become unnecessary, although its
availability should be clearly indicated in the event of necessity.***

•   •   •

On September 30, 1963, WMCA's case was significantly strength-
ened by the filing of an amicus curiae brief by Archibald Cox, United
States Solicitor General. As noted earlier, a brief filed by the Department of Justice has a twofold importance: First, as a product of
an organization possessed of talent and resources unmatched by all
but the very largest private law firms, its arguments are usually of
high quality; second, and perhaps even more important, it represents
the considered judgment of the executive branch of the United States
Government—a judgment which the Supreme Court, as a coordinate
member of the national government, is not likely to ignore or consider
lightly.

Quite understandably, WMCA was elated by the government's decision to intervene. On October 1, 1963, Straus announced in an
editorial:

WMCA—and you—gained a friend in court this week. The U.S.
Government officially joined our appeal to the Supreme Court for a
fair apportionment of the New York Legislature. On behalf of the
federal government, Solicitor General Archibald Cox charged that

* Author's italics.

our state's legislature is rigged so as to "discriminate egregiously" in favor of rural voters.

. . . The Solicitor General describes the privileged folk upstate as "a favored class of voters with powers disproportionate to their members."

The Solicitor General, unlike the other parties attacking New York's apportionment, proceeded "on the assumption that the Fourteenth Amendment *permits* reasonable deviations from equal per capita representation in at least one house of the legislature." However, "any *substantial* discrimination in per capita representation constitutes," Cox argued, "a denial of equal protection of the laws unless it bears a reasonable relation to some permissible objective of legislative apportionment."

The constitutional weakness of New York's apportionment scheme, the brief continued, resulted from the fact that its "systematic discrimination in per capita representation is based upon *irrelevant,* even invidious, criteria. . . . [New York's system of apportionment] stands unmasked as deliberate discrimination against the urban voter, in favor of the rural voter, designed to preserve minority rule. To deprive a man of a vote or to denigrate the value of his vote just because he lives in the city rather than the country is an arbitrary discrimination wholly foreign to democratic ideals."

Moreover, the Solicitor General asserted:

The notion that any particular "community of interest" should be accorded greater voting strength than the number of people comprising the community warrants is inconsistent with basic democratic ideals. *If one minority, such as rural voters, is to be guaranteed greater political power, there is no reason why other minorities, such as labor union members, businessmen, Catholics, Negroes, suburbanites, slum-dwellers, and persons over 65,* could not claim similar rights. The argument made on behalf of appellees [New York State] comes down to the proposition that a state should be free to select a particular minority for preferential treatment in voting without any criteria whatever for making the selection. And if it may favor one, it may repress another. This, we submit, is the very essence of the arbitrariness that both equal protection and due process condemn.

"In short," Cox concluded, "both houses of the New York Legislature substantially discriminate against citizens living in populous areas. New York offers no reasons justifying such substantial discrimination. The apportionment therefore violates the Fourteenth Amendment."

New York State replied on October 18, 1963. The two major arguments contained in Assistant Solicitor General Galt's brief were that: "New York's formula for apportioning its legislature is entirely consistent with the Fourteenth Amendment; this case presents no occasion for the intervention of federal equity power."

EXCERPTS FROM THE STATE'S BRIEF

A. *The standard under the Fourteenth Amendment.*

    1. *The lesson of Baker* v. *Carr: Governments must be responsive to the popular will.*

We share appellants' [WMCA] concern that all men should have equal voice in the councils of government. Our democratic tradition demands no less of us. *But it is quite another matter to espouse a doctrine of per capita* representation as being the sole test of equality. . . .

Obviously, there are factors other than per capita representation which determine whether one citizen has a voice in the legislature "equal" to that of another citizen. As this Court itself noted, "to assume that political power is a function exclusively of numbers is to disregard the practicalities of government. . . ."

      •   •   •

The principle that governments must be responsive to the popular will, unlike that of per capita representation, is one that certainly commands the backing of our democratic traditions and is fundamental to the workings of our institutions. It would be entirely appropriate to measure the structure of any state legislature against this ideal. Such a principle would do no violence to the freedom of each state to determine for itself the best way to guarantee each voter an equal opportunity to be heard in the legislature. And—equally important— it would focus the attention of the Court on the genuine evil, which is not that state legislatures depart from per capita representation but that they often depart from the limits set on them by the people themselves.

. . .

3. *The role of other devices for assuring that government rests on the consensus of the governed.*

The role of the many traditional factors which go into an apportionment has been widely disparaged and misunderstood. . . . The important value is that each citizen . . . should have equal access to the legislative process so that the legislature may be responsive to his needs.

. . .

B. *New York's formula is constitutional.*

. . .

2. *The New York formula provides for representation which is responsive to the popular will and at the same time prevents domination of the state by any one locality.*

. . .

First, New York emphasizes that many of the interests which a citizen may wish to assert in the legislative process are interests which touch on his relation to the government of his country as well as to the state, and that these interests consequently are often peculiar to the citizens of one county and its government.

. . .

The many functions performed by the county in New York State today reflect both the historic gravitation toward the county as the central unit of political activity and the realistic fact that, as the largest government units, the county is usually the most efficient and practical medium for initiating and carrying out programs beneficial to residents of the different areas of the state. . . .

. . .

. . . To perform its functions effectively, the county needs a representative in the legislature who can represent its interests and bring its needs to the attention of the entire body. By the same token, the legislature must know the needs and problems of all the areas of the state. Unless there were some guarantee of minimum representation to the electors of a single county, the less densely populated counties would be grouped together in multi-county districts in which the legislator's functions as a liaison between the county and state government would virtually disappear.

.   .   .

Second, New York has emphasized in its apportionment formula that the physical size of a district may have a significant bearing on a voter's capacity to influence the legislative process through his elected representative. If a per capita standard resulted in the creation of overly large districts in sparsely populated areas, a voter in such a district would be disadvantaged in two ways: (1) he would not have the intimate contact with his legislator possessed by a voter in a heavily populated district covering a relatively few city blocks—distance might prevent the voter from expressing his views to the legislator and the legislator from consulting his electorate; (2) a voter in an overly large district would be likely to lose one of the most important benefits of a single-member district system—representation in a district which has some modicum of shared problems, enabling the legislator to become a spokesman for views which might not otherwise be heard. If a district spans too large an area, there may well be no such community of interest among its voters, and one of the most important links between a citizen and the legislative process will have disappeared.

.   .   .

Third, New York must take into account the unique concentration of population and political power in a few localities in order to assure that the wishes and needs of the rest of the state will not be ignored.

.   .   .

The time for another apportionment argument was drawing near —this one before the Supreme Court. When the Court agreed to hear WMCA's appeal, it did the same for three other apportionment cases from Alabama, Virginia and Maryland. The Court also scheduled all the oral arguments for successive days in mid-November. Sand explained:

The way the Court was treating the apportionment cases indicated that it felt the issue was not one to be handled in a piecemeal fashion. Therefore, the lawyers representing the plaintiffs in these four cases met together twice, early in November. This was important so that arguments would not be advanced which were advantageous to one plaintiff but disadvantageous to the other plaintiffs.

The four states involved made no similar attempts to coordinate their arguments. "We sent copies of our brief to those states that requested one," Assistant Solicitor General Galt commented, "but we developed our own defenses and held no conferences with any other states."

Since 1962, when *Baker* v. *Carr* was decided, two changes in Supreme Court membership had taken place. Justices Whittaker and Frankfurter had resigned, and been replaced by Justice Byron White, 47, and Justice Arthur Goldberg, 56,* respectively.

Byron R. White, the youngest man on the Court, had a most unusual career prior to his appointment to the bench. During his college days at the University of Colorado, he was an All-American football star. It was while playing professional football that he gained the nickname, "Whizzer," because of his extraordinary athletic prowess. After spending a year at Oxford as a Rhodes Scholar, he entered Yale Law School where he graduated first in his class. In 1946 he became Chief Justice Fred Vinson's law clerk and, between 1947 and 1960, practiced law in Denver. In 1960, he served as Colorado campaign manager for John F. Kennedy in his race for the presidency. The following year he served the Kennedy administration as deputy attorney general and in 1962 was appointed to the Supreme Court by President Kennedy. On the Court he has become known as a "swing man," a justice who ideologically is placed near the center of the Court and who thus casts an important vote in close decisions.

Arthur J. Goldberg, is a graduate of Northwestern University. He was a well-known labor lawyer, having served as general counsel to the United Steelworkers of America and the industrial union department of the AFL-CIO. In 1961 he became Kennedy's Secretary of Labor and was noted for his extremely active and successful interven-

* Ages at the time the *WMCA* case was heard.

tion in labor disputes. In 1962, President Kennedy appointed him to the Supreme Court. Justice Goldberg quickly established himself as a member of the most liberal, activist wing of the Court. Together with Justices Black and Douglas, he exhibited utmost concern with the preservation of civil liberties. After the death of Adlai Stevenson, in 1965, he became the United States Ambassador to the United Nations.

7

How the
Supreme Court Decides

An astute observer, analyzing the reception the Court was likely
to give to arguments on the apportionment issue, might have sized up
the positions of the justices as follows: Chief Justice Earl Warren
and Associate Justice Brennan were known for their vigorous efforts
on behalf of individual rights and could be expected to view
sympathetically claims that urban citizens were being discriminated
against; Justices Black and Douglas, in *Colegrove* v. *Green,* the
Illinois apportionment case, had taken the position that weighting
votes in favor of rural inhabitants was a violation of the Fourteenth
Amendment; Justice Clark, who had been prepared to decide *Baker*
on its merits, clearly believed an apportionment to be unconstitutional
if it could be demonstrated to be arbitrary or irrational; Justice
Stewart had cautiously indicated support of Clark's position; Justice
Harlan unquestionably would support any apportionment which
could, by the furthest stretch of the imagination, be considered rational; Justice Goldberg, because of his general record in support of
civil liberties and his normal alignment with Black and Douglas might
logically be placed with those two justices; and White, the most
"middle-of-the-road" justice was likely to adopt Clark's "rationality"
test and be guided by the particular facts of each apportionment case.
The odds, then, favored WMCA's test case.

The way in which the justices of the Supreme Court make a decision can best be understood by first noting the procedures the Supreme Court follows in deciding a case.

The Court begins work in October and alternates two-week periods
of hearing cases with two-week periods of recess. Argument sessions

run from Monday through Thursday, and each litigant is normally allowed one hour to present his case. Friday, the justices sit in conference. The period of recess is devoted to opinion writing and the study of appeals and certiorari petitions (requests for the Court to grant review of lower court decisions).

Justice Clark, in a speech delivered before the American Bar Association, has given an admirable inside account of how conference sessions are conducted:

> Let us go from the austere courtroom—from the friezes depicting the lawgivers, the Greek Ionic columns and the heavy draperies—to the oak-paneled conference chamber and see what is going on there. Over the mantel facing the large rectangular conference table is a portrait of Chief Justice [John] Marshall, the fourth Chief Justice by number, but the first in stature. Around this table are nine chairs, each bearing the nameplate of a member of the Court. At the east end sits the Chief Justice, and at the west, Mr. Justice Black, the senior associate justice. On the sides, in order of seniority, sit the remaining associate justices. Bookcases from floor to ceiling line the walls containing all the opinions of the federal courts. Here the Court meets in conference at 11:00 A.M. on each Friday during or preceding an argument week, and rarely does it rise before 5:30 P.M.
>
> Only the justices are present at conferences. There are no clerks, no stenographers, no secretaries, no pages. This long-established practice is based on reason. The Court must carry on these Friday conferences in absolute secrecy, otherwise its judgments might become prematurely known and the whole process of decision destroyed. We therefore guard its secrets closely. There must be no leak. Scores of years ago the Court was convinced that there was a leak. At that time two page boys waited on the justices within the conference room. After considerable investigation it was decided that the only possible leak was through one of these lads. After all, no one else was present save the justices! So, since that day, no page—no person other than the justices themselves—has ever attended a conference. . . .
>
> Upon entering the conference room, each justice shakes hands with those present, another custom dating generations back. We first take out our assignment sheets or lists for the day. . . .
>
> What type of cases come up for discussion? First, appeals, then petitions for certiorari, next *informa pauperis* cases [petitions filed by

individuals who cannot afford to hire a lawyer], and, more important than all, the cases argued previously in the courtroom. The Court always decides the latter cases the same week in which they were argued. . . .

The Chief Justice starts the conference by calling the first case on the list and then discussing it. He then yields to the senior associate justice and on down the line seniority-wise until each justice who wishes to be heard has spoken. There is no time limitation. The order is never interrupted nor is the speaker. . . .

After discussion of a case a vote is taken. We each have available a large docket book, evidently, from its appearance, handed down to us by the first of the justices. It has a hinge on its fly-leaf which is kept locked. There we keep a record of the votes. Ever since John Marshall's day the formal vote begins with the junior justice and moves up through the ranks of seniority, the Chief Justice voting last. Hence the juniors are not influenced by the vote of their elders! . . .

· · ·

After the vote is recorded in argued cases there remains the task of writing the opinion for the Court. At the conclusion of the conference the cases are assigned for writing. The Chief Justice assigns those in which he has voted with the majority and the senior justice voting with the minority the remainder. . . .

When one starts to write an opinion for the Supreme Court of the United States he learns the full meaning of the statement of Rufus Choate that "one cannot drop the Greek alphabet to the ground and pick up the *Illiad*." It takes the most painstaking research and care. Mr. Justice Cardozo was not far wrong when he said, "a Judge must be a historian and prophet all in one." In the average case an opinion requires three weeks work in preparation. When the author concludes that he has an unanswerable document, it is printed in the print shop in the Supreme Court building and circulated to each of the justices. Then the fur begins to fly. Returns come in, some favorable and many otherwise. In controversial cases, and all have some touches of controversy, the process often takes months. The cases are often discussed by the majority both before and after circulation. The final form of the opinion is agreed upon at the Friday conferences. Of course, and justice may dissent or write his own views on a case. These are likewise circulated long before the opinion of the majority is announced. . . ."

The role of the oral argument itself is authoritatively described by Justice Harlan:

> . . . I think that there is some tendency at the trial bar . . . to regard the oral argument as little more than a traditionally tolerated part of the appellate process. The view is widespread that when a court comes to the hard business of decision, it is the briefs, and not the oral argument, which count. . . .
>
> . . . I think that the lawyer who depreciates the oral argument as an effective instrument of appellate advocacy, and stakes all on his brief, is making a great mistake. There are several reasons for this.
>
> First of all, judges have different work habits. There are some judges who listen better than they read and who are more receptive to the spoken than the written word.
>
> Secondly, the first impressions that a judge gets of a case are very tenacious. They frequently persist into the conference room. And those impressions are actually gained from the oral argument, if it is an effective job. . . .
>
> Thirdly, the decisional process in many courts places a special burden on the oral argument. . . . In the Supreme Court, our practice, as is well known, has been to hold our conferences at the end of each week of arguments. . . .
>
> Fourthly, and to me this is one of the most important things, the job of courts is not merely one of an umpire in disputes between litigants. Their job is to search out the truth, both on the facts and the law, and that is ultimately the job of the lawyers, too. And in that joint effort, the oral argument gives an opportunity for interchange between court and counsel which the briefs do not give. For my part, there is no substitute, even within the time limits afforded by the busy calendars of modern appellate courts, for the Socratic method of procedure in getting at the real heart of an issue and in finding out where the truth lies.
>
> Now, let me turn for a moment to some of the factors which seem to me to make for effective oral arguments. The art of advocacy— and it is an art—is a purely personal effort, and as such, any oral argument is an individualistic performance. Each lawyer must proceed according to his own lights, and if he tries to cast himself in the image of another, he is likely to become uneasy, artificial and unpersuasive. But after you make allowance for the special talents of individuals, their different methods of handling arguments, their dif-

ferent techniques, it seems to me that there are four characteristics which will be found in every effective oral argument, and they are these: *First,* what I would call selectivity; *second,* what I would designate as simplicity; *third,* candor; and *fourth,* what I would term resiliency. Let me address myself briefly to each.

By "selectivity," I mean a lawyer's selection of the issues to be argued. There is rarely a case which lends itself to argument of all of the issues within the normal time limitations upon oral argument. . . .

Most cases have one or only a few master issues. In planning his oral argument the wise lawyer will ferret out and limit himself to the issues which are really controlling, and will leave the less important or subordinate issues to the Court's own study of the briefs. Otherwise, one is apt to get tanglefoot, and the Court is left pretty much where it began.

The next thing I refer to is "simplicity." Simplicity of presentation and expression, you will find, is a characteristic of every effective oral argument. In the instances where that quality is lacking it is usually attributable to one or two reasons—lack of preparation or poor selection of the issues to be argued. There are some issues that do not lend themselves to oral argument as well as they do to written presentation. The preparation of an oral argument is a good deal more than merely making a short form summary of the briefs. An oral argument which is no more than that really adds nothing to a lawyer's cause.

The process of preparation that the appellate advocate undergoes involves, *first,* the selection of the issues he will argue; *second,* a marshalling of the premises on which those issues depend; *third,* planning the structure of his argument; and, *fourth,* deciding how he shall express his argument. It is sometimes forgotten by a lawyer who is full of his case, that the Court comes to it without the background he has. And it is important to bear this in mind in carrying out the preparation for argument in each of its phases. Otherwise the force of some point which may seem so clear to the lawyer may be lost upon the Court.

The third thing which is of the essence of good advocacy is "candor." There is rarely a case, however strong, that does not have its weak points. And I do not know any way of meeting a weak point except to face up to it. It is extraordinary the number of instances one sees where through a question from the Court or the argument of one's adversary a vulnerable point is laid bare, and the wounded lawyer ducks, dodges and twists, instead of facing up to the point four square. Attempted evasion in an oral argument is a cardinal sin. No answer to an embarrassing point is better than an evasive one. With the Court, lack of candor in meeting a difficult issue of fact or of law goes far to destroying the effectiveness of a lawyer's argument, not merely as to the point of embarrassment, but often as to other points on which he should have the better of it. For if a lawyer loses the confidence of the Court, he is apt to end up almost anywhere.

The fourth and final thing which I have suggested goes to the root of a good oral argument is "resiliency." For some reason that I have never been able to understand, many lawyers regard questioning by the Court as a kind of subversive intrusion. And yet, when one comes to sit on the other side of the bar, he finds very quickly that the answer made to a vital question may be more persuasive in leading the Court to the right result than the most eloquent of oral arguments. I think that a lawyer, instead of shunning questions by the Court, should welcome them. If a court sits through an oral argument without asking any questions, it is often a pretty fair indication that the argument has been either dull or unconvincing.

I am mindful, of course, that the Court's privilege of asking questions is sometimes abused, and that the price a lawyer has to pay is some interruption in the continuity of his argument, and perhaps some discomfiture, and in extreme instances perhaps never getting through with what he had planned to say. And yet, I think that the price is well worth what the lawyer may have to pay in the loss of the smooth-flowering quality he would like his argument to have. A lawyer can make no greater mistake, I assure you, in answering questions by the Court if he attempts to preserve the continuity of his argument by telling the judge who asks the question that he will come to it later. Usually, he never does. Or in saying, "Judge, I have dealt with that in my brief." Even if the lawyer does come back to the question later on, the force of his answer, if it is a good one, and often also of his arguments in other aspects where he perhaps is in a stronger position, is usually lost—at least upon the judge who has asked the question.

On November 12 and 13, 1963, *WMCA* was argued. The New York apportionment case was the first considered by the Court. Leonard Sand and Archibald Cox, the United States Solicitor General, were each allotted one hour for oral argument; Assistant State Solicitor General Irving Galt was allotted two hours to argue in behalf of New York.

EXCERPTS FROM THE ORAL ARGUMENT
BEFORE THE SUPREME COURT

The Chief Justice: November 20, *WMCA, Inc., appellants,* versus *John P. Lomenzo, Secretary of State for the State of New York, et al.*

The Clerk: Counsel are present.

The Chief Justice: Mr. Sand.

Mr. Sand: Mr. Chief Justice, may it please the Court. Before turning to the special details of this, the New York legislative apportionment case, a word or two might be appropriate concerning the relationship which this case bears to the body of cases decided by lower federal courts and by the state courts since this Court's decision in *Baker* v. *Carr.*

It is fitting that the Court today begins its review of some of these cases with the New York apportionment case because the New York case reflects one extreme of judicial reaction to *Baker* v. *Carr.*

In this case the Federal District Court in the Southern District of New York sustained the constitutionality of the apportionment of a state legislature in which challenge was directed to both houses of the legislature and in which both houses of the legislature were seriously malapportioned.

Following *Baker* v. *Carr* with surprising speed and near unanimity a consensus appears to have been reached by the lower federal district courts and by the state courts, and that consensus is that regardless of what rule may apply to the second house of a legislature, surely one house must be apportioned primarily on the basis of population.

• • •

Mr. Justice Stewart: You talk about one house and both houses as though there is something constitutionally inevitable about a state having a bicameral legislature.

Mr. Sand: Every state except Nebraska has a bicameral legislature.

Mr. Justice Stewart: Is there any reason why they shouldn't have a tricameral legislature?

Mr. Sand: I know of no such reason.

Mr. Justice Stewart: Or of a [state] having a unicameral legislature?

Mr. Sand: Every state could have a legislature consisting of as many houses as it saw fit.

Mr. Justice Stewart: Is there any reason why a state need have any legislature at all?

Mr. Sand: I think the state must have some body.

.   .   .

Mr. Justice Goldberg: Do you think philosophically restraints upon what a majority may do run consistent with our democratic theory?

Mr. Sand: Mr. Justice Goldberg, I think that relates to the nature of the restraint. Of course . . . restraints may be placed upon majorities, but I do not believe that it lies within the power of a state to select any minority within that state and to confer upon that minority majority status.

Mr. Justice Harlan: Where do you find that in the Constitution?

Mr. Sand: I find that in the Equal Protection Clause.

.   .   .

Mr. Sand: I would like to turn, if I may, to the apportionment itself, to the formula which we challenge, and the challenge is directed to the formula itself.

Mr. Justice Harlan: What you are going to say now, I take it, is all premised on the proposition that the Equal Protection Clause requires a state to apportion or to approach apportionment—let me put it that way—approach apportionment from a population basis. Is that right?

Mr. Sand: It requires something less than that, Mr. Justice Harlan, because our position is that the beginning point, the starting point to measure the validity of a particular apportionment is the extent to which it bears a relationship to the population of the state.

Mr. Justice Harlan: I think before you get into the question of the apportionment you ought to address yourself to what the Constitution standard is, if any.

Mr. Sand: But let me say that in New York—

Mr. Justice Harlan: The federal Constitution standard. In order to make your argument based on statistics, figures which you call malapportionment, meaningful from the standpoint of this Court you have got to address yourself to the question of what the federal Constitution standard is against which the apportionment has got to be judged.

Mr. Sand: And I say, Mr. Justice Harlan, that that federal standard prohibits a state from selecting a minority group within that state regardless of the nature of that minority, whether it be based on race or any other basis.

Mr. Justice Harlan: Not on race. This is a question of the distribution of power, not a question of restriction on individual voting rights. This is a question of the distribution of power, governmental power in the state.

Mr. Sand: This, as appellants see it, is a question of whether an individual who is a member of a class whose votes are discounted because the legislature has selected some other group and has given to that other group a preferred position and additional power, whether a member of such a class has individual rights enforceable under the Fourteenth Amendment.

Mr. Justice Harlan: I know, Mr. Sand, but to make my question concrete, what is there in the federal Constitution that says that a state cannot apportion its Senate in the same way, if it chooses to, that the United States apportions Senators among the various states?

I recognize the arguments that are made as to the federal analogy not being an analogy. But what is there in the federal Constitution, in the Fourteenth Amendment more specifically, that says that a state cannot allot Senators on the basis of geographical communities as distinguished from population?

Mr. Sand: The concept of equality of all people within a state, and we are dealing here with the most basic civil liberty which those people have.

Mr. Justice Harlan: Those are words. Tell me where it is that you find that in the Constitution?

Mr. Sand: I find that in the implications of the Equal Protection Clause of the Fourteenth Amendment as suggested by this Court in *Baker* v. *Carr* and as exists by analogy in the decision and language of this Court in *Gray* v. *Sanders*.

Mr. Justice Harlan: Of course you agree that *Baker* v. *Carr* furnishes no light, no guidance to what you are debating here?

Mr. Sand: Except, Mr. Justice Harlan, the applicability of the Equal Protection Clause to questions of legislative apportionment, and from that flows everything else that I have urged on this Court.

Mr. Justice Harlan: You are taking an awful big jump.

•   •   •

Mr. Justice Harlan: Supposing New York said we think it will be a desirable thing to give labor unions a Senator. Would that be unconstitutional?

Mr. Sand: I believe it would, Mr. Justice Harlan.

Mr. Justice Harlan: Or management, or both. Do you think that would be unconstitutional?

Mr. Sand: I would say this at a minimum. When the net result of applying whatever formula the state devises is to produce a legislature, the members of which are elected on a basis which is radically disproportionate to population, the burden then shifts to the state and the state must then come in and say we have adopted this method of apportioning our legislature because we feel it more effectively represents the people.

I don't think this Court need forever close the door upon experimentation by states.

Mr. Justice Harlan: Then I am putting the question to you: Supposing the State of New York said explicitly to you—supposing the State of New York said explicitly we will have one member of the Senate allotted to the so-called business interests in the state and another member allotted to the so-called labor interests in the state.

Mr. Sand: And if the net result of that was to cause there to be a legislature, the members of which did not represent population, it would be unconstitutional.

Mr. Justice Harlan: In my hypothesis I am assuming that neither of those norms would have taken into account any population figure.

Mr. Sand: What I mean to suggest by the form of my reply, Mr. Justice Harlan, is that nobody is saying that because the legislature must be apportioned to population we throw out the map of the state, we disregard natural boundaries, we disregard political subdivisions. The legislature may consider all of this, may consider more.

But in apportioning representatives on the basis of these criteria the net result must be a legislature which proportionately represents population, and when it does not, then at a minimum the burden is upon the state to come forth and to say we have adopted this method because this method achieves greater representativeness of the legislature.

Now that is not what New York State has done.

Mr. Justice Stewart: Mr. Justice Harlan has asked you unsuccessfully. Maybe nobody can successfully answer it. Where does this rule of law come from that you have just enunciated?

Mr. Sand: I think it comes from the basic nature of our system, the genius of our democratic society. These are words, but these are concepts which are very meaningful. These are concepts which are in the basic traditions of democratic—

Mr. Justice Stewart: Are you assuming a majority rule in each legislative district, that it is constitutionally required for example?

Mr. Sand: I don't understand.

Mr. Justice Stewart: Well, let's take a senatorial district in New York, and let's say that the candidates are A and B, the red party and the green party. Well, then A gets 55% of the votes and B gets 45% of the vote. So the green party, all those thousands and thousands of green voters are not represented by Mr. A in the state legislature, are they?

Mr. Sand: They are not, that is correct, absent some form of proportional representation.

Mr. Justice Stewart: When you get to talking about majority rule what happens to this? And now let's say in the very next legislative district the other party, the green party wins by 55%. Now those 45% in the contiguous district, red party voters, are not represented by Mr. B from that district in the legislature, are they?

Mr. Sand: No, this is an inherent result of—

Mr. Justice Stewart: Is there some political, if subtle, reality in having the disenfranchised A voters in district one be more or less represented by the A voters who prevailed in district two?

I am only suggesting, Mr. Sand, and it is simply a suggestion, that the problems we have before us in these cases this week are somewhat more complicated and subtle than has been suggested in the briefs, and that they cannot necessarily be solved by simple eighth grade arithmetic.

•　　•　　•

Mr. Justice Goldberg: Mr. Sand, doesn't your argument come down to this: that apportionment to carry out equal protection, which by its very terms presupposes equality among voters, must be basically according to population; that if a state wants to deviate from that basic constitutional concept of equality it must give a good reason, there must be a good reason? And then you read the opinions of this Court and you find out race isn't a good reason, occupation—that was the question Justice Harlan put to you—occupation under analogous cases couldn't be a good reason. And now you are confronted with the question which you are arguing, or whether the place where you happen to live within the state, residence, whether it is on a farm, in the city, you believe is not a good reason? Isn't that what it comes down to?

Mr. Sand: That is exactly the position, Mr. Justice Goldberg. . . .

* * *

With leave of the Court, I would reserve the balance of my time.

The Chief Justice: Mr. Solicitor General.

Mr. Cox: Mr. Chief Justice, may it please the Court, this case is one of the four arising from New York, Alabama, Maryland and Virginia that would require the Court to rule for the first time upon the constitutionality of the apportionment of seats in the state legislature.

The ultimate question to which all four cases point is what is the meaning in the field of legislative apportionment of the constitutional guaranty of equal protection of the law, or, to put it a little differently, by what standards, by what criteria giving meaning to the phrase "equal protection" is the constitutionality of a legislative apportionment to be judged?

Neither these cases nor any other single case or group of cases can supply the complete answers to the ultimate question.

We need to keep the ultimate question in mind, however, because whatever is decided here must fit a coherent analysis as has been suggested in the argument and must be susceptible of being reduced to generalizations that are good across the board.

But, at the same time, this could be made a manageable problem I think only by adhering to the traditional process of deciding the cases before the Court and other questions that logically don't have to be decided to the future, provided they can genuinely be left open and nothing is said that necessarily determines them.

* * *

Mr. Justice Stewart: What bothers me, Mr. Solicitor General—it has bothered me all morning—is that you say "if" a state can do this, "if" a state can give heavier representational weight to a seaport and so on.

Now isn't it conceivable that perhaps one state in the particular context of the social, economic and political conditions of that state might and another state might not be able to constitutionally?

I mean what has North Dakota got in common with New York? What does New Mexico have in common with Maine? I don't know yet. I would suggest this Court may not know the answer. And you may not know the answer, with all the local problems in these various areas.

Mr. Cox: That's quite true. All I was attempting to say, Mr. Justice, is that the crazy quilt rule won't supply a complete answer to the cases unless there are some limits on what interests a state may prefer over other interests.

．   ．   ．

Mr. Justice Goldberg: Suppose that the motive of the legislature was to attract population to an underpopulated part of the state because they felt that was necessary for the economic development of the state.

．   ．   ．

Can a state adopt a deliberate policy of trying to get its people not to congregate in the big cities with the traffic problems, school problems?

Mr. Cox: I think it may do that by some means and not others.

In other words, Mr. Justice, I fully recognize that in enacting tax laws and regulatory laws, granting appropriations or other benefits, that a state may encourage one industry or discourage another or protect the wage earner or the management, and so forth.

Mr. Justice Goldberg: Can't they select a legislature on the basis that will carry out the very thing that a legislature does?

Mr. Cox: No, I exclude that.

I would say that—and coming again quite slowly—there is nothing novel in my suggestion that bases of classification that will do in one area of state action may be impermissible in another.

Let me come back to your case—

Mr. Justice Goldberg: But if I may interrupt for a moment, so you can focus on this: If the state is permitted to do all these things to carry out state objectives, which things can only be done through the legislature, why cannot the state then design the legislature to achieve the permissible objectives?

．   ．   ．

Mr. Cox: In matters of apportionment I suggest the critical difference is between rules which serve the purpose of making representative government work better, the operation of which may have the collateral consequence of creating discriminations per capita, and rules whose only function is to create classes of voters with preferred political rights disproportionate to their number, which we say is impermissible.

·   ·   ·

At noon a brief recess was taken and then promptly at 12:30 p.m. the Court reconvened. After the Solicitor General finished his hour, Mr. Galt was called.

> *The Chief Justice:* Mr. Galt.
>
> *Mr. Galt:* Mr. Chief Justice and may it please the Court, I would like to lose no time in coming down directly if I may to what appears to be a basic difference of opinion as to an issue which is cardinal I think to the determination of the case.

·   ·   ·

I think it's beyond argument, listening to the appellants, reading their briefs, that they equate per capita representation with equality of representation. And here we disagree emphatically.

We only agree to the extent that we believe there should be equality of representation. But what does that term connote?

We see no necessary correlationship between per capita representation and equally of access to the legislative process.

We don't regard per capita representation as the test, as the only test, or as the starting point.

Basically I think the difficulty lies in the question of the conception of a constituency and the functions and purposes of a single member district system.

·   ·   ·

> *Mr. Justice Harlan:* Your argument and your brief as I read it all proceed from the premise that the measure, the constitutional standard, against which these conflicting views have to be judged is found in the Equal Protection Clause in the Fourteenth Amendment. You accept the proposition, do you?
>
> *Mr. Galt:* We of necessity, in view of the *Baker* decision, of course

accept the proposition that the Fourteenth Amendment, the protection clause of the Fourteenth Amendment, is applicable to—

Mr. Justice Harlan: There is room for *Baker* to operate even though you object to that proposition. You recognize that, don't you?

. . .

Mr. Galt: Without accepting the proposition that the Equal Protection Clause applies to apportionment cases?

Mr. Justice Harlan: Yes.

Mr. Galt: I think the *Baker* case made it expressly applicable to apportionment cases. The question is whether apportionment will fit in to the condemnation of the Equal Protection Clause, and here we say —Pardon me?

Mr. Justice Harlan: That is the question I am putting to you, whether the Equal Protection Clause in the field of apportionment, the abstract notion of equal protection as embodied in the Fourteenth Amendment, applies to apportionment, that is, distribution of governmental power within a state, as distinguished from its obvious application in relation to racial discrimination to bar industrial voting rights.

Mr. Galt: It certainly, I think, can apply, and the question then will be whether the well recognized, well developed standards under the Equal Protection Clause condemn the apportionment system.

Mr. Justice Harlan: That's all right. I just wanted to get the premise of your argument.

Mr. Galt: Yes. But assuredly we contend most vigorously that the Equal Protection Clause when viewed against the rationale that we will be discussing certainly will not and should not strike down New York's system in any respect.

. . .

. . . [A]s to New York we will show that the state had a perfect right consistent with every concept of federal constitutionality to take into consideration a number of factors and not to be limited by per capita representation either as the sole standard or as the starting point of inquiry.

. . .

The Chief Justice: To what extent is population important in this field?

Mr. Galt: No particular weight as such can be ascribed to population or any other factor. Nor is it necessary to use any of the specific factors we have mentioned. The question is these factors being available, these factors being useful to accomplish the legitimate purposes of a single member district system, whether or not their use or lack of use is done in such a way as to offend under the standards of this clause the requirements of equal protection as explicitly made applicable to apportionment cases.

Mr. Justice Harlan: If the population hasn't anything to do with it or nothing particularly to do with it, where does the lack of equal protection come?

Mr. Galt: Well, the lack of equal protection would come in, taking again Mr. Justice Brennan's [majority] opinion [in *Baker*]. If there is a legislature which had done like Tennessee had done, sixty or seventy years had gone by, and they do not stick to their constitution—

Mr. Justice Harlan: You haven't got that situation here. . . .

Mr. Galt: That's right, we do not have that situation.

Mr. Justice Harlan: Then in answering the Chief Justice's question you said the population didn't have anything to do with it, didn't have anything controlling to do with it. Then if you take population out what is left of the equal protection argument?

Mr. Galt: The question was what weight had to be attached to it, and I merely suggested it wasn't a matter of attaching any preconceived notion of so much weight to the per capita standard, so much weight to the question of one representative per county. It is not a question of that at all.

Where population might under certain circumstances enter into the picture as in a case like Tennessee, for example, where because of all these developments it has become a crazy quilt without rhyme or reason, it is that kind of failure to observe the standards set forth in the state constitution, that kind of situation where the legislature locks itself into power and people literally can do nothing, which is not New York. It is that kind of situation that you may very well find that you are led to the situation where there is no policy but arbitrary and capricious, paraphrasing, of course, Mr. Justice Brennan's language in *Baker*. We have a crazy quilt without rhyme or reason, borrowing Mr. Justice Clark's language.

But there is no particular weight to be ascribed to any of these ingredients. Any or all of them may well belong in any well-balanced apportionment system. Certainly the states have a right to use, if they so desire, criteria other than population as the prime standard, or one from which certain deviations are permitted.

*   *   *

The Court recessed at 2:30 p.m. and reconvened at 10:10 a.m., Wednesday, November 13, 1963, with Galt continuing his oral argument.

*   *   *

Mr. Justice Goldberg: General, is it not a concept of a republican form of government—I am not saying now that the Constitution mandates it in a particular instance—but isn't it a basic underlying concept of republican government that an equal number of people, for example, ought to have an equal number of representatives, equality of that type?

Mr. Galt: In a single constituency, yes.

Mr. Justice Goldberg: Let's not talk now about technical—I mean isn't it the basis of a republican type of government that when you pick a representative that your participation in that process ought to be equal to your neighbors, and so on?

Mr. Galt: Certainly with the underscoring, Mr. Justice Goldberg, that there are sharp clashes of opinion epitomized in the case as to what constitutes equality.

*   *   *

Now, I'd like to advert in the short time remaining to one or two other things.

We were talking yesterday or I started to talk yesterday about the reasons why federal equity power should not be used to intervene. [There are] no compelling circumstances. And the very same factors which in our view bear on the validity of the New York formula on its merits also suggest there is no reason for intervention of federal equity power.

Without repeating them in detail, they are per capita representation, clear control of the legislature by urban counties, built-in opportunity for the majority to convene a constitutional convention, and the consistent adherence by the legislature to principles, standards embodied in its constitution. All of these suggest there is absolutely no warrant here for federal equity intervention and that you have to look to the governmental processes of New York as a whole since the question of legislative apportionment, after all, is only one facet of the problem of giving citzens of the state an adequate voice in state government.

·   ·   ·

The responsiveness to the popular will is not to be measured by giving any one element any particular specific weight. It is to be measured by the realities of the situation with regard to all of the factors which we do have in the State of New York.

I see that my time has expired, and, unfortunately, I must leave the rest of my remarks.

8

One Man, One Vote

While awaiting the decision of the Supreme Court, radio station WMCA maintained a steady attack upon Governor Rockefeller's alleged indifference to the needs of city residents. On January 12, 1964, Straus denounced the Governor's annual message to the legislature and assured his listeners that thanks to the radio station's efforts in their behalf, their interests would soon be better protected. Rockefeller's obvious eagerness to become the Republican party's candidate for the presidency in 1964 made him a particularly attractive target for Straus' not so subtle verbal attacks. As painted by Straus, the Governor was the picture of an overly ambitious politican, ruthlessly prepared to further his own career even at the expense of defenseless children:

> The first rule of Republican politics is that a governor must have a balanced budget if he wants to run for President. And so Governor Rockefeller just had to submit a balanced budget for New York.
> First he wrapped up a bundle of tax and other gimmicks good for this year only. Then he did what comes naturally when money's tight in New York State: He swindled New York City.
> Though the city has always gotten far less than its fair share of state aid, the Governor now wants to cut us down some more.
> And the victims hardest hit will be the kids in our public schools. Last year the state spent over a hundred dollars more on each school child upstate than it spent in the city. But this year the spread will be even greater.
> That's what it's costing our children to help Nelson Rockefeller run for President.

On February 17, 1964, the Supreme Court unleashed some verbal blows of its own, and if Straus' remarks made Rockefeller wince, the Court's seemed likely to rout its victims. By a 6-3 vote, the Court held in *Wesberry* v. *Sanders* that as far as practicable, *congressional* districts must contain an equal number of people.

Justice Hugo L. Black delivered the opinion of the Court. Black, at 78, was the oldest, but by no means the least vigorous member of the Court. An avid tennis player, he reputedly selected his law clerks as much on their ability to serve as challenging tennis partners as on their capacity to perceive the subtle elements of a complex legal issue. A graduate of the University of Alabama, Black began practice as a police court judge in Birmingham and later served as a prosecuting attorney in Jefferson County, Alabama. In 1927, he began the first of his two terms as a United States Senator and, during the depression, became widely known for his zealous support of New Deal legislation. He was appointed to the Supreme Court by President Roosevelt in 1937 and was immediately the subject of a scandal when his one-time membership in the Ku Klux Klan became known. Despite this inauspicious beginning, Black has successfully established himself as one of the most dedicated champions of civil liberties and minority-group rights ever to sit on the Court. He is best known for his belief that the provisions of the Bill of Rights should be interpreted literally, with no compromises for the professed requirements of national security. An extreme activist, Black fearlessly attacks all efforts by national or local governments to infringe upon what he considers to be the constitutionally protected rights of individuals.

After noting the severe population inequalities which characterized Georgia's congressional districting and asserting that the Court had the power to decide issues involving the validity of congressional districting, Black went straight to the central issue: the constitutional limitations imposed upon the freedom of states to apportion representatives as they wished.

We hold that, construed in its historical context, the command of Art. I. sec. 2, that representatives be chosen "by the people of the several states" means that as nearly as is practicable one man's vote in a congressional election is to be worth as much as another's.

Radio station WMCA took no editorial notice of the decision. Nevertheless, the decision did seem to have bearing upon WMCA's own case. *Wesberry,* of course, dealt only with the question of *congressional* districting; WMCA was, in fact, attacking a *state* apportionment. However, the broad principle enunciated by the Court that fundamental to the "ideas of democratic government" lay the principle of one man, one vote, logically was as applicable to the New York situation as to Georgia's. The one catch was that the Court had used Article I of the Constitution, not the Equal Protection Clause, as the justification for its ruling. Article I refers exclusively to Congress; the Fourteenth Amendment refers to questions of wholly internal state actions as well. However, it must be realized that the Court did not reject the possibility that Georgia's apportionment could be invalidated on equal protection grounds as well as on the first article. In a footnote to his opinion, Black explicitly commented: "We do not reach the arguments that the Georgia statute violates the Due Process, Equal Protection, and Privileges and Immunities Clauses ["No State shall make or enforce any law which shall abridge the privileges or immunities of citizens of the United States. . . ."] of the Fourteenth Amendment." Whether the Equal Protection Clause imposed a one man, one vote standard on *state* apportionments still awaited adjudication.

Finally after several months, the Supreme Court did indeed announce its opinion in the New York apportionment case. As recalled by WMCA attorney Leonard Sand:

Peter Straus and I were both anxious to be in court when the *WMCA* decision was announced. In late May and early June, we tried to be in Washington on Opinion Mondays [until 1965, the Supreme Court always announced its decisions on Mondays] if our schedules permitted. When we could not be there, the facilities of WMCA and its affiliate, Radio-Press International, were geared to get word of any decision to us promptly on its announcement. WMCA knew that the

96   *ONE MAN, ONE VOTE*

one news story on which it could not be scooped was a decision in the
WMCA case.

Peter and I were both in Westchester on the morning of June 15
and Peter telephoned and suggested that we meet at the Westchester
County Airport and fly to Washington in the Straus Broadcasting
Group plane which Peter pilots himself. We knew that there were
probably only two more Opinion Mondays and two groups of important cases undecided—apportionment and sit-ins—and that it was
unlikely that both groups of cases would be decided on the same day.
June 15 looked like a 50-50 chance to be the day.

In the cockpit of the plane going down to Washington, Peter and I
talked about timing. We had in our previous discussion exhausted the
subject of merits and of the likelihood of victory. We were both
extremely optimistic of victory. But how soon would the Court require
the states to act? The real question we concluded is what the Court
would say about timing in the light of the experience in implementing
the school segregation cases. "All deliberate speed" had proved to be
a troublesome phrase given the reluctance of some state officials ever
to comply with the Court's interpretation of the Equal Protection
Clause. What formula of words would the Court now invoke to advise
state governments of the rate of speed at which they must end malapportionment?

Sand and Straus soon had their answer. On the afternoon of June
15, 1964, the Court, in a series of decisions dealing with the apportionment provisions of six states—Alabama, Colorado, Delaware,
Maryland, New York and Virginia—held that "as a basic constitutional standard, the Equal Protection Clause requires that the seats
in both houses of a bicameral state legislature must be apportioned
on a population basis." WMCA had won its case!

The decisions were delivered by the Chief Justice. Earl Warren is a
graduate of the University of California. Active in local government,
he served as district attorney of Alameda County, California, from
1925 to 1939. He then became attorney general of California and
gained recognition by playing an active role in influencing the federal
government to force all citizens and inhabitants of Japanese origin to
leave the state during World War II. Between 1943 and 1953 he was
Governor of California, being elected to office for an unprecedented

three terms. In 1953 at the age of 62 he was appointed Chief Justice by President Eisenhower. On the Court, Warren has been most noted for his ability to influence his colleagues to submerge their differences and take a united stand in such important and sensitive issues as *Brown* v. *Board of Education,* the school segregation case of 1954. Ideologically, Warren must be characterized as a moderate liberal who is deeply concerned with individual liberties, but who is not prepared to take as extreme libertarian positions as Associate Justices Black, Douglas, and Goldberg.

In the New York case, *WMCA* v. *Lomenzo,* the Chief Justice after reviewing the history of WMCA's litigation, and describing the formulas by which the state was apportioned concluded that: "The weight of the votes of those living in populous areas is of necessity substantially diluted in effect."

The philosophic justification for the Court's ruling that both houses of a state legislature must be apportioned substantially on a population basis was outlined by the Chief Justice in the Alabama companion case, *Reynolds* v. *Sims.* Warren began by noting the importance of the right to vote and the effect of weighted voting upon that right. "*Wesberry* clearly established that the fundamental principle of representative government in this country is one of equal representation for equal numbers of people, without regard to race, sex, economic status, or place of residence within a state," the Chief Justice pointed out. Clearly, Warren continued, "Our problem, then, is to ascertain, in the instant cases, whether there are any constitutionally cognizable principles which would justify departures from the basic standard of equality among voters in the apportionment of seats in state legislatures."

Logically, in a society ostensibly grounded on representative government, it would seem reasonable that a majority of the people of a state could elect a majority of that state's legislators. To conclude differently, and to sanction minority control of state legislative bodies, would appear to deny majority rights in a way that far surpasses any possible denial of minority rights that might otherwise be thought to result. Since legislatures are responsible for enacting laws by which all citizens are to be governed, they should be bodies which are collectively responsible to the popular will. . . . With respect to the allocation of legislative representation, all voters, as citizens of a state, stand in the same relation regardless of where they live. Any suggested criteria for the differentiation of citizens are insufficient to justify any discrimination, as to the weight of their votes, unless relevant to the permissible purpose of legislative apportionment. Since the achieving of fair and effective representation for all citizens is concededly the basic aim of legislative apportionment, we conclude that the Equal Protection Clause guarantees the opportunity for equal participation by all voters in the election of state legislators. . . ."

Warren was not impressed with the argument that, because one house of Congress, the Senate, was not apportioned on a population basis, the states should also be allowed to apportion one house of their bicameral legislatures on non-population bases. The Chief Justice rejected the federal analogy, arguing that the historical circumstances of the origin of Congress and state legislatures was dissimilar. Moreover, to permit one house to be apportioned on a non-population basis would impede majority rule:

The right of a citizen to equal representation and to have his vote weighted equally with those of all other citizens in the election of members of one house of a bicameral state legislature would amount to little if states could effectively submerge the equal-population principle in the apportionment of seats in the other house. If such a scheme were permissible, an individual citizen's ability to exercise an effective voice in the only instrument of state government directly representative of the people might be almost as effectively thwarted as if neither house were apportioned on a population basis. Deadlock between the two bodies might result in compromise and concession on some issues. But in all too many cases the more probable result would be frustration of the majority will through minority veto in the house not apportioned on a population basis, stemming directly from the failure to accord adequate overall legislative representation to all of the state's citizens on a nondiscriminatory basis. In summary, we can perceive no constitutional difference, with respect to the geographical distribution of state legislative representation, between the two houses of a bicameral state legislature.

The Chief Justice hastened, however, to assure the states that it was not the Court's intention to undermine or destroy their bicameral forms of government:

> We do not believe that the concept of bicameralism is rendered anachronistic and meaningless when the predominate basis of representation in the two state legislative bodies is required to be the same —population. A prime reason for bicameralism, modernly considered, is to insure mature and deliberate consideration of, and to prevent precipitate action on, proposed legislative measures. Simply because the controlling criterion for apportioning representation is required to be the same in both houses does not mean that there will be no differences in the composition and complexion of the two bodies. Different constituencies can be represented in the two houses. One body could be composed of single-member districts while the other could have at least some multi-member districts. The length of terms of the legislators in the separate bodies could differ. The numerical size of the two bodies could be made to differ, even significantly, and the geographical size of districts from which legislators are elected could also be made to differ. And apportionment in one house could be arranged so as to balance off minor inequities in the representation of certain areas in the other house. In summary, these and other factors could be, and are presently in many states, utilized to engender differing complexions and collective attitudes in the two bodies of a state legislature, although both are apportioned substantially on a population basis.

The Court made clear that the rule of one man, one vote need not be applied with mathematical exactness or precision. What was less certain, however, was to what extent states might accommodate nonpopulation factors in their apportionments without violating the Court's prescription. "For the present," Warren said, "we deem it expedient not to attempt to spell out any precise constitutional tests. What is marginally permissible in one state may be unsatisfactory in another, depending on the particular circumstances of the case. Developing a body of doctrine on a case-by-case basis appears to us to provide the most satisfactory means of arriving at detailed constitutional requirements in the area of state legislative apportionment."

The final point to be considered by the Court was what action the lower federal courts should take once they determined that a state's apportionment was unconstitutional. Addressing himself specifically to the New York State situation, the Chief Justice said:

> Since all members of both houses of the New York Legislature will be elected in November, 1964, the court below, acting under equitable principles, must now determine whether, because of the imminence of that election and in order to give the New York Legislature an opportunity to fashion a constitutionally valid legislative apportionment plan, it would be desirable to permit the 1964 election of legislators to be conducted pursuant to the existing provisions, or whether under the circumstances the effectuation of appellants' right to a properly weighted voice in the election of state legislators should not be delayed beyond the 1964 election.

Justice Harlan dissented in all six cases, Justice Stewart in the Colorado, Maryland and New York cases, and Justice Clark in the Colorado and New York cases.

Justice Stewart, in a dissent joined by Justice Clark, excoriated the Court's decision, charging that the ruling was inconsistent with the provisions of the Constitution and inconsistent with the proper role of the judiciary. Stewart described what he considered to be the proper constitutional standards to be applied in apportionment cases:

> . . . [T]he Equal Protection Clause demands but two basic attributes of any plan of state legislative apportionment. First, it demands that, in the light of the state's own characteristics and needs, the plan must be a rational one. Secondly, it demands that the plan must be such as not to permit the systematic frustration of the will of a majority of the electorate of the state.

Stewart then considered New York's apportionment in light of the constitutional standard which he had elaborated. He emphasized that New York's was a rational plan, reflecting a policy which accorded major emphasis to population, some emphasis to region and community, and a reasonable limitation upon massive overcentralization of power. "What the state has done," Stewart concluded, "is to adopt a plan of legislative apportionment which is designed in a rational way to ensure that minority voices may be heard, but that the will of the majority shall prevail."

Justice Clark, in a separate dissent, took exception to the Court's application of the one man, one vote principle to both houses of a state legislature. In his view, "if one house is fairly apportioned by population . . . then the people should have some latitude in providing, on a rational basis, for representation in the other house." The concept of federalism, Clark reminded the Court, requires that only irrational and arbitrary state actions or provisions should be invalidated.

Justice Harlan wrote a long and scholarly dissent, delving deep into the language, proposal and ratification, and subsequent history of the Fourteenth Amendment in order to support his assertion that the Court's ruling had no basis in the federal Constitution. His research, he concluded, proved that:

. . . [T]he Equal Protection Clause was never intended to inhibit the states in choosing any democratic method they pleased for the apportionment of their legislatures. This is shown by the language of the Fourteenth Amendment taken as a whole, by the understanding of those who proposed and ratified it, and by the political practices of the states at the time the amendment was adopted. It is confirmed by numerous state and congressional actions since the adoption of the Fourteenth Amendment, and by the common understanding of the amendment as evidenced by subsequent constitutional amendments and decisions of this Court before *Baker* v. *Carr* made an abrupt break with the past in 1962.

The failure of the Court to consider any of these matters cannot be excused or explained by any concept of "developing" constitutionalism. It is meaningless to speak of constitutional "development" when both the language and history of the controlling provisions of the Constitution are wholly ignored. Since it can, I think, be shown beyond doubt that state legislative apportionments, as such, are wholly free of constitutional limitations, save such as may be imposed by the Republican Form of Government Clause [Const., Art. IV, sec. 4: "The United States shall guarantee to every state in this Union a republican form of government. . . ."], the Court's action now bringing them within the purview of the Fourteenth Amendment amounts to nothing less than an exercise of the amending power by this Court. . . .

Harlan concluded his dissent on a somber note, pessimistically predicting that the Court's decision would undermine the strength of federalism and constitutional government:

> With these cases the Court approaches the end of the third round set in motion by the complaint filed in *Baker* v. *Carr*. What is done to-day deepens my conviction that judicial entry into this realm is profoundly ill-advised and constitutionally impermissible. . . . I believe that the vitality of our political system, on which in the last analysis all else depends, is weakened by reliance on the judiciary for political reform; in time a complacent body politic may result.

9

Congress vs. the Court

Press reaction to the Reapportionment Cases was generally favorable. Anthony Lewis of the New York *Times* called the Supreme Court ruling "a decision of historic importance. . . . Not since the school segregation cases 10 years ago," Lewis stated, "had the Court interpreted the Constitution to require so fundamental a change in this country's institutions."

Although the Supreme Court had emphasized that it was protecting personal rights, not group interests, commentators viewed the decisions primarily in political terms. In an article in the June 16 New York *Times* entitled "South Faces Era of Vast Changes," Claude Sitton predicted that the Court's ruling would "speed racial change and the growth of a two-party system in the South." While most political analysts agreed that the probable nation-wide effect of the decisions would be to transfer political power from rural to urban and suburban areas and to facilitate the enactment and enforcement of "progressive" legislation, Roscoe Drummond of the New York *Herald Tribune* suggested that the ruling would prove to be a boon to conservative principles.

Reaction to the decisions was not uniformly favorable, however. Professor Thomas W. Christopher of the University of North Carolina (now dean of the law school, University of New Mexico), in a letter printed in the June 28 edition of the New York *Times,* asserted that:

> The Supreme Court decision that a state legislature must be apportioned by population alone raises questions both as to its soundness and as to whether the justices have gone astray in their views of the Court's authority.
> The decision is anti-liberal—it is reactionary. Many people, includ-

ing this writer, believe that urban voters are not adequately represented in many state legislatures, and we would fight for and vote in
a referendum for relief. But this would be in a democratic vote and we
would abide by the judgment of the majority in a fair election.

.   .   .

A distressing aspect of the decision is that it expresses a lack of
confidence not only in the people to rule themselves on this point but
also in future justices to correct abuses. I had thought that the people
were entitled to experiment and even to make mistakes. I am one of
those who have stood up for the Court down where the battle is, but
here it has forgotten itself.

Professor Christopher was not alone in his dissatisfaction. A con-
certed effort quickly developed in Congress to overturn the Supreme
Court's decision and, in fact, to curb sharply the power of the Court
itself. In an article in the July 9 *Wall Street Journal,* Joseph W. Sullivan described the struggle taking place in Congress.

REDISTRICTING UPSET?

*Drive in Congress Tries
To Guard Rural Power
In State Legislatures*

---

*Efforts Seek to Nullify Court
Edict that Apportionment
Be Only on Population Line*

But Action May Be Too Late

Big-city folks beware: Irate rural and small-town forces in Congress are moving to block your prospects for gaining a bigger voice in
the state legislatures.

And while it would take a bolt of legislative lightning for them to
succeed in the short time remaining before Congress is due to adjourn
for fall campaigning, a high-powered effort is in the making and success cannot be ruled out.

.   .   .

Proposed antidotes mostly take the form of constitutional amendments providing for apportionment of at least one legislative chamber
along some other lines, usually geographical. But their sponsors, wary
of delays in getting an amendment ratified, are casting about for even
more potent correctives. Emerging as their favorite: A simple but almost unprecedented act of Congress stripping the federal courts of
their authority to pass on state apportionment matters. In the end,
some combination of the two approaches may be embraced.

.   .   .

Arrayed behind the House push is an almost implausible coalition of
Republicans, Southern Democrats and a significant sprinkling of liberal
Northern Democrats from the hinterlands of such states as California,
Pennsylvania and Ohio. Its high command takes in such perennially
feuding partisans as Democratic Majority Leader [Carl] Albert of
Oklahoma, his GOP counterpart, Rep. [Charles B.] Halleck of Indiana,
and the grand marshall of Southern resistance forces, Democratic
Rep. [Howard W.] Smith of Virginia. . . .

Welding their alliance is a mutual fear that the Supreme Court's
apportionment mandate will sap the political influence of their home
districts in state governments. According to calculations by the National Municipal League, a voice of city government, strict allocation
of state legislative power along population lines would bring more
than 30 state capitols under urban and suburban domination, up from
less than 10 at present.

The possibilities implicit in such a transformation, including a
reslicing of state revenues to satisfy city appetites for more schools and
superhighways, more solicitude for labor and less for the farmer,
have not been lost on rural and small-town envoys in Congress. Buf-
feting the Congressmen's own political moorings, in addition, is the
fact that many state party organizations are built on legislative-district
cells; many lawmakers fear attaching more cells to the cities and
fewer to the countryside would lower their rank in the state party hier-
archy. An even greater worry among some big-state Republicans is
that augmented urban power, favoring city Democrats, may weaken
entire state GOP structures.

.   .   .

H. J. Res. 1055, introduced June 24 by Representative William M. McCulloch of Ohio, a Congressman usually considered a staunch ally of the Court, received the most attention. It read, in a significant part:

> Nothing in the Constitution of the United States shall prohibit a state, having a bicameral legislature, from apportioning the membership of one house of its legislature on factors other than population, if the citizens of the state shall have the opportunity to vote upon the apportionment.

Far more radical was H.R. 11925, the proposal of Representative ("Judge") Howard W. Smith of Virginia. Introduced on July 2, it was designed to strip the federal courts of their jurisdiction in state apportionment cases:

> The Supreme Court shall not have the right to review the motion of a federal court or a state court of last resort concerning any action taken upon a petition or complaint seeking to apportion or reapportion any legislature of any state of the Union or any branch thereof.
>
> •   •   •
>
> The district courts shall not have jurisdiction to entertain any petition or complaint seeking to apportion or reapportion the legislature of any state of the union or any branch thereof.

By August 19, a total of 138 bills and resolutions had been offered in the House by ninety-nine authors. In the Senate, principal attention centered on a proposal offered by Senator Everett Dirksen of Illinois, Republican minority leader. It was explicitly designed to postpone for as long as four years the exercise of jurisdiction by all federal courts over all apportionment matters. It provided that:

> Upon application made by or on behalf of any state or by one or more citizens thereof in any action or proceeding in any court of the United States, or before any justice or judge of the United States, in which there is placed in question the validity of the composition of either house of the legislature of that state or the apportionment of

the membership thereof, such action or proceeding shall be stayed until the end of the second regular session of the legislature of that state which begins after the date of enactment of this section.

Dirksen was quite frank as to his intentions. "I trust," he said, "that [the bill] will be referred forthwith to the Committee on the Judiciary. That committee will meet tomorrow morning, and I apprehend that, even without the benefit of witnesses, we may be able, as an emergency matter, to have the bill reported forthwith. Then I shall undertake to have it taken off the calendar and, in the form of an amendment, offer it to a bill in which I think it will have the best chance."

The first stage of Dirksen's prediction soon came to pass. As caustically noted by Dean Robert B. McKay of New York University:

. . . [T]he Judiciary Committee solemnly deliberated the matter on August 4 for forty-five minutes (presumably denied more expeditious action by the objections of Senators Quentin N. Burdick of North Dakota and Philip A. Hart of Michigan, who alone dissented) and reported S. 3069 favorably on that day. Senator Dirksen then promptly made his decision to attach S. 3069 as a rider to the foreign aid authorization bill (H.R. 11380), the pending business of the Senate, which had been clearly designated as "must" legislation.

The speed with which the committee approved the measure elicited angry response from the press and the professors. On August 6, the New York *Times,* in an editorial, sharply pointed out:

Whatever may be said in favor of Senator Dirksen's move for a Congressional mandate delaying application of the Supreme Court order to reapportion state legislative districts on a "one man, one vote" basis, there can be no question that he is wrong in seeking to stampede it through Congress without full consideration of its damaging potentialities.

Time for national contemplation of the sweeping implications of the Court's decision, which is the Dirksen bill's immediate aim, has much to commend it. But haste on Capitol Hill is a perilous corrective for the perils the Court's critics see in too hasty effectuation of its reapportionment ruling. Certainly a bill raising such grave questions of the division of authority between the legislative and judicial branches ought not be railroaded through as an irrelevant rider to foreign aid appropriations. This is legislative blackmail, not deliberation.

On August 10, fifteen law school deans and professors voiced their opposition to the court-curbing measures in Congress. The text of the telegram they sent to Senators Mike Mansfield of Montana and Everett Dirksen of Illinois read:

> The undersigned law school professors and deans oppose the pending proposal, offered by Senator Dirksen and others, to require all federal courts to stay action for two to four years in legislative apportionment cases.
> We object to this and similar proposals, entirely apart from the merits of the recent Supreme Court decisions on apportionment, because the legislative approach unwisely and indeed dangerously threatens the integrity of our judicial process.
> The effect of these proposals is not, as has sometimes been said, merely to limit the jurisdiction of the federal courts. It is to declare by statute, without constitutional amendment, that for a period of time certain constitutional rights may not be vindicated in any court, state or federal. . . .

Perhaps more important than these protests was the fact that a group of "liberal" Senators decided to "speak at some length," in Senator Wayne Morse's phrase, in opposition to the Dirksen proposal. Their "baby" filibuster began to take effect. On August 12, Deputy Attorney General Nicholas Katzenbach, Solicitor General Archibald Cox and legal aides of Senators Dirksen and Mansfield met. As a result of their all-day conference, a slightly amended version of Dirksen's proposal was offered. As the debate continued, opponents of court-curbing gained powerful support. On August 18, E. W. Kenworthy of the New York *Times* reported that "the Democratic mayors of several large cities [Richard J. Daley of Chicago, James Tate of Philadelphia, Joseph Barr of Pittsburgh, Jerome P.

Cavanaugh of Detroit, John F. Collins of Boston, Herman W. Gold-
ner of St. Petersburg, Fla., and Raymond R. Tucker of St. Louis]
are getting into the congressional battle over legislation to delay or
nullify the Supreme Court ruling on apportionment of state legislatures." Their strategy, according to Kenworthy was to pressure
President Lyndon Johnson into opposing the Dirksen proposal.

The mayors were not the only people interested in what President
Johnson's position was. In an August 19 article in the New York
Daily News, Ted Lewis gave voice to this concern:

> As President Johnson has been mighty positive previously in his
> stand on key legislative issues before Congress, his reluctance to speak
> out in the controversy over the Supreme Court's reapportionment de-
> cision seems out of character.
>
> His silence has been explained as due to his belief that the issue is
> a congressional matter. Yet, up until now, he has never hesitated to
> intrude in legislative affairs to get things done.
>
> As President, of course, he may not want to associate himself either
> for or against the present effort to override, through legislation, the
> Court's edict against delays in reapportionment of state legislatures on
> a popular vote basis. To do so would perhaps suggest that he is ques-
> tioning the co-equal status of the judicial branch, and the "Warren
> Court" in particular.
>
> The net result of Johnson's effort to keep aloof from the con-
> troversy has been to further confuse an already badly confused legis-
> lative situation.

On August 19, the New York *Herald Tribune* published the results of a Gallup Poll on national reaction to the Supreme Court's
decisions in the apportionment cases. Gallup reported that public
opinion supported the Court by a 3-2 margin. Significantly, the sur-
vey pointed out, "in the nation's largest cities—those with 500,000
population or more—opinion is heavily in favor of the court's ruling.
In the smallest communities—those under 2,500—the weight of
opinion is on the disapproval side."

August 19 also marked the passage of the Tuck Bill. As reported
by the *Wall Street Journal* of August 20:

The House, launching a frontal assault on the Supreme Court, approved a bill that would nullify the Court's authority to order state legislatures to reapportion.

By a vote of 218 to 175, the House approved without dilution a plan by Rep. [William M.] Tuck (D., Va.) for stripping all federal courts of jurisdiction over state legislative seating.

•   •   •

The effect of Rep. Tuck's measure, far more stringent than the moratorium on court-ordered reapportionment proposed by Sen. Dirksen (R., Ill.), would be to quash all past Supreme Court edicts in this field. That takes in not only its ruling of two months ago that districts in both houses of state legislatures must be equal in population but also its more limited 1962 decision establishing federal court purview in instances where both houses of a legislative body are malapportioned.

•   •   •

Supporting the measure were 122 Republicans and 96 Democrats, mostly from the South but including a sprinkling of Northerners from thinly populated areas. A group of 35 city and suburban-area Republicans joined 140 liberal Democrats in opposition.

•   •   •

The House action, after an unruly five-hour debate, carried strong overtones of a squeeze by Republican strategists to make the Senate swallow the milder Dirksen plan. While stating that they would have preferred some softer remedy, House Minority Leader [Charles] Halleck of Indiana and his chief lieutenants opposed all softening proposals brought before the House. GOP ranks joined with Southern Democrats to shout down an amendment by Rep. [Charles Raper] Jonas (R., N.C.) that embodied the very delaying mechanism once advocated by Mr. Dirksen and Mr. Halleck jointly. The modified Dirksen plan currently before the Senate was also rejected by voice vote, and Rep. [Chet] Holifield (D., Calif.) was shouted down when he attempted to tack on language taken from the Fourteenth Amendment guaranteeing "the equal protection of the laws."

•   •   •

Shortly after the Tuck Bill passed the House, Congress adjourned to allow the Democrats and Republicans time to hold their Presidential Nominating Conventions. The Republicans, who met first, called for a constitutional amendment to limit the apportionment decisions. The Democrats, however, at the insistence of President Johnson, took no position on the issue. Anthony Lewis, reporting in the August 23 edition of the New York *Times,* revealed that the President thought any attempt to deal with the question of apportionment at the convention would only inflame feelings and make the problem harder to handle in Congress:

> "Never try to kill a snake until you have the hoe in your hand," one White House aide said. He was putting into a Texas phrase the President's belief that proper tactics in Congress, not public talk, will blunt the attack on the Court.

On September 8, Senator Dirksen moved to cut off the liberals' "baby" filibuster: He filed a cloture petition. During the short debate on the cloture motion, Senator Frank Church of Idaho succinctly summarized the arguments against the court-curbing measure:

> I have concluded that, regardless of how one approaches it, the Dirksen rider is wrong. It is wrong to force a vote upon it without benefit of committee hearings; it is wrong to attach it to the foreign aid bill, where it has no place, and thus to coerce the consent of the President. But, above all, it is wrong on its merits, because it seeks to suspend the Constitution of the United States as that document relates to the right of each citizen to have representation in his state legislature which is as equal as possible to that of all other citizens of his state.
>
> I do not believe that it is within the power of the Congress to suspend the Constitution either in this, or any other particular. If the Dirksen rider were to pass, I believe that it would be promptly struck down by the courts. The folly of our action would then be matched by its futility.

In reply, Senator Dirksen said:

> It has been alleged on the floor, and in editorials, that this is an attack on the Court. I could use an inelegant term to describe those

allegations. But I shall content myself with saying that nothing could be further from the truth. . . .

The amendment before the Senate is a breather. It is nothing more. We had no choice on the question. Our resolution [for amendment of the Constitution] was submitted, but how could we do something about it before the present session of the Congress adjourned?

He rejected as insufficient, however, a "sense of Congress" resolution which had been offered as an alternative by Senators Jacob K. Javits of New York, and Hubert H. Humphrey and Eugene J. McCarthy of Minnesota. That measure read:

It is the sense of the Congress that in any action or proceeding in any court of the United States or before any justice or judge of the United States in which there is placed in question the validity of the composition of any house of the legislature of any state or the apportionment of the membership thereof, adequate time should be accorded (1) to such state to conform to the requirements of the Constitution of the United States relating to such composition or apportionment consistently with its electoral procedures and proceedings and with its procedure and proceedings for the amendment of the constitution of such state, and (2) for consideration by the states of any proposed amendment to the Constitution of the United States relating to the composition of the legislatures of the several states, or to the apportionment of the membership thereof, which shall have been duly submitted by the Congress to the states for ratification.

Dirksen responded to this proposal with heavy-handed ridicule:

Is it not wonderful for this legislative, coordinate branch of the government to get on its knees and say to the Court, "Please, Mr. Court, be gracious, be graceful. Let us give them adequate time"? We are asked to beg a little. I do not propose to beg, because that demeans the dignity and authority of this branch of government.

The cloture motion was decisively defeated by a note of 30-63. Immediately thereafter, however, a motion to table the Dirksen rider was also decisively defeated, this time by a 38-49 vote. The explanation for the difference in outcome of these two votes lies in an issue extraneous to the question of apportionment: The Senate liberals had been supported by Southern Senators in the vote against cloture for fear of its being used against them in civil rights votes; free to vote according to their normal inclinations, the Southerners deserted the liberals to vote overwhelmingly against tabling the Dirksen rider.

The debate on the court-curbing measures soon lost its sharpness and by September 23, Senator Mansfield, who had originally supported Dirksen, candidly noted:

> It is clear that there is not the substantial majority which is necessary to invoke cloture on the Dirksen-Mansfield amendment. It is also clear that there is not a majority to table the amendment. . . .
>
> . . . The leadership lives in the hope that one day reason will be permanently enshrined in this body and that the rules will be used and not abused, whether the issue is civil rights or reapportionment or whatever. There is only one reasonable way to redeem the reputation of the Senate in this kind of situation. That is by the adjustment of positions. . . .

Adjustment of positions did in fact take place. The following day the Senate passed a substitute amendment by a 44-38 vote. The Mansfield measure read:

> It is the sense of Congress that:
> (a) In any action in any district court of the United States in which the constitutionality of the apportionment of representation in a state legislature or either house thereof is drawn in question, any order affecting the conduct of the state government, the proceedings of any house of the legislature thereof, or of any convention, primary or election could properly, in the absence of unusual circumstances, including those which could make unreasonable or embarrassing demands on a state in adjusting to the requirements of the Court's order,
>   (1) allow the legislature of such state the length of time provided for a regular session of the legislature plus thirty days, but not to exceed six months in all, to apportion representation in such legislature in accordance with the Constitution, and
>   (2) permit the next election of members of the state legisla-

ture following the effective date of this act to be conducted in accordance with the laws of such state in effect
on September 20, 1964.

(b) In the event that a state fails to apportion representation in
the legislature in accordance with the Constitution within the
time granted by any order pursuant to this section, the district
court having jurisdiction of the action shall apportion representation in such legislature among appropriate districts so as
to conform to the constitution and laws of such state insofar
as is possible consistent with the requirements of the Constitution of the United States, and the court may make such further
orders pertaining thereto and to the conduct of elections as
may be appropriate.

The liberals had won a decisive victory.

Dan Cordtz, writing in the September 25 edition of the *Wall Street
Journal,* analyzed the entire districting struggle in great detail:

ANATOMY OF A FILIBUSTER

How Liberals Succeeded in Scuttling Delay on Districting

The filibuster, reviled by the many and revered by the few, scored
sweet victory in the Senate yesterday—a triumph made more flavorful
by the irony attached to it.

For those Senators who defeated the Dirksen proposal to delay
state legislative reapportionment by talking it to death (an innocuous
substitute was accepted) are those same liberals who have been trying for years to de-fuse the filibuster as the powerful weapon of an
intransigent minority.

What's more, the liberals' success comes at a time when filibusters
seemed, on the record at least, to be losing their punch. Twice in
the last two years the Senate has halted debate by invoking cloture.
By contrast, the procedure had succeeded only four times in 26 attempts
during the previous 45 years.

The irony of the situation was not lost on either the winners or the
losers. A leader of the filibuster forces said afterwards, a trifle sheep-
ishly, "Well, if we can't get rid of the thing, at least we can show
them how it ought to be used."

His remark, and the manner in which he made it, illustrate the
mixed feelings shared by those who talked to death the ill-fated rider

introduced Aug. 12 by Senate Minority Leader Dirksen (R., Ill.).
While mildly embarrassed by their use of a device they have frequently
assailed in the past, most also feel a boyish delight in having walloped
the enemy with its own club. Declares Sen. Hart (D., Mich.), only
partly in jest: "Maybe we'll have to reconsider our feelings about
filibusters."

But if the matter of who did the talking is intriguing, more important
is this question: In light of the failure of other recent filibusters, against
the communication satellite and civil rights legislation, why and how
did this one succeed?

In the corridors of the Capitol, there are almost as many suggested
answers as Senators queried. One that can quickly be rejected is any
contention the victory was the result of a clearly conceived, smoothly
executed master plan. In fact, the progress of the battle was characterized more than anything else by miscalculation and, at times,
ineptitude.

In retrospect, it now seems obvious that both President Johnson
and Majority Leader Mansfield (D., Mont.) failed completely to gauge
the relative potential strength on both sides of the issue. Convinced
that Sen. Dirksen had the whip hand and in order to head off what
he feared would be an even tougher amendment, the President permitted two high-ranking Justice Department officials to help draft the
rider. Worse, these administration lawyers told the Minority Leader
his measure was constitutional—a curbstone opinion he quoted often
during the weeks of debate.

For his part, Sen. Mansfield not only lent his name as co-sponsor of
the amendment (reluctantly, by his own testimony), but assured Sen.
Dirksen he would have no part in any efforts to kill or replace it. A
rigidly honorable man, the Majority Leader steadfastly lived up to his
agreement until Sen. Dirksen released him, even though he had concluded earlier the rider could no longer be enacted. The liberals remain
convinced that without Sen. Mansfield's help, the Dirksen amendment
would have been killed long ago.

If the administration and the Senate leadership overestimated Sen.
Dirksen's strength, however, it must be added that so did those who
challenged him. The decision of half-a-dozen Senators to launch what
seemed to be a futile fight was not, for a long time, based on any con-
viction they could win. "The best we hoped for, initially anyway, was
that we could hold things up long enough for the White House to reverse itself," one now recalls.

Ironically, the reversal never came—in public, at least. "The White House attitude shifted from active cooperation with Dirksen to benevolent neutrality toward us," according to an aide of a filibuster leader.

To the gratified surprise of the tiny group that began the campaign, however, their numbers slowly grew even without the blessings of the Administration. Sen. Hart believes that many Senators were convinced because the liberals managed to portray the issue as one of constitutionality. "It's inherent in our system that the Supreme Court occasionally will make decisions that offend the majority of the people," he declares. "If Congress starts acting as the agent of the outraged majority in cutting down the Court, it will completely undermine our constitutional relationship." Realization of what was ultimately at stake, says Sen. Hart, persuaded several men who were out of sympathy with the Court's one-man, one-vote decision.

Still others, on the other hand, were impressed by more practical considerations. More than two out of three Americans now live in areas loosely defined as urban or suburban, the regions which stand to gain most from early implementation of the Supreme Court decisions on reapportionment. And while it took time for representatives of these political subdivisions to make themselves heard, their indignant clamor was effective when it came.

Especially helpful, according to Sen. [Paul] Douglas (D., Ill.), were the forceful statements of their views made by big-city politicians at the Democratic National Convention. After that sobering encounter, more than one Democratic Senator reassessed his own position.

Whatever the weight of the cities' influence, Sen. Mansfield recalls that there was a discernible shift of feeling in the Senate when it reconvened after the convention recess. In retrospect, Sen. Dirksen agrees that the tide probably began to turn against him then. He has a different explanation, however.

According to the Minority Leader's hindsight analysis, it was then that time—on which he had counted as an important ally—started working for the other side. His clever parliamentary ploy, attaching the reapportionment measure as a rider to the veto-proof foreign aid bill, could only be effective while Congress faced an imminent adjournment. Once that preconvention deadline had fallen by the way, there was no longer a very convincing case for hasty action.

As a consequence, a few uneasy Senators who would have hesitantly backed the Dirksen amendment immediately after its introduction, had time for second thoughts. It was their vote that turned his attempt to invoke cloture into a debacle and put the handwriting on the wall in letters no one could ignore. But the Illinois Republican had committed himself to a cloture vote before the Democratic convention and could not back out without conceding his weakness. So the vote was held and, when they saw the needed two-thirds majority would not be attained, Southern Democrats on whom Sen. Dirksen had counted instead maintained their traditional position of opposing cloture. Not even the liberals believed the 63-30 defeat truly represented Senate sentiment on the Dirksen amendment, but Sen. [William] Proxmire (D., Wisc.) now counts that crushing vote as the point at which the Dirksen forces lost the fight.

Public opinion, parliamentary maneuvers, the force of important political pressure groups and even the weight and logic of debate on the Senate floor—all these, then, played a role in the final decision. As one of the filibuster leaders sums it up:

"What it all proves, I think, is that unless the country feels very strongly in favor of a certain piece of legislation, it can be beaten—and that's as it should be. There was never any real groundswell of public opinion in favor of the Dirksen amendment. In fact, we think feeling was against it. In any case, that's what careful Senate deliberation is all about."

Important as reapportionment is, Sen. Dirksen nevertheless says philosophically: "You need a highly emotional issue, like civil rights, or a bill with lots of appeal (Comsat) to get cloture. Otherwise, any determined group can make a filibuster work. It's as simple as that."

10

Back to the District Court

In New York State, news commentators predicted that the Democratic party would gain power as a result of the Supreme Court's decision in *WMCA* v. *Lomenzo*. Douglas Dales, in an article in the June 16 New York *Times* noted that "the Supreme Court's action came as a major blow to the Republican party, which has relied on apportionment formulas written into the Constitution to maintain its control of the legislature." Dales continued, "Some have regarded the legislative formulas as the bulwark of Republican power in the state."

Democratic party officials hailed the Court's ruling. Mayor Robert F. Wagner said:

> Today's historic decision represents a turning point in the governmental history of our state. In clear language the nation's highest Court has affirmed a long held contention that the state's major cities were the victims of gross inequities in their representation in Albany.
>
> I trust that swift action will be taken to implement this important decision. The City of New York is proud of its role in bringing this decision about, and grateful for the efforts of radio station WMCA in bringing this matter before the courts.

William H. McKeon, state Democratic committee chairman, called the decision:

> A great victory for the American people. It has been unfortunate that the Governor and the Republican party in this state persisted in fighting a losing battle to continue a 70-year-old injustice which discriminated against many.

Republican comments upon the decision were less enthusiastic. Governor Rockefeller noted tersely, "I am confident that following study and analysis an apportionment plan for the legislature will be developed as promptly as possible." James Desmond, in the June 19 edition of the New York *Daily News,* reported that State Senate Majority Leader Walter J. Mahoney had stated that there would be no special session of the legislature to reapportion New York's legislative seats.

Emphasizing that a half dozen legal staffs—from the Governor's office, top legislative committees of both houses and the Attorney General's office, among others—were still studying the Supreme Court decision," Desmond related, "Mahoney offered a personal, off-the-cuff opinion that the federal district court won't press reapportionment for the coming election.

Mahoney pointed out that the Supreme Court decision left standing the New York law that provides for the nomination of legislative candidates at primary elections, a compelling reason for delay. The state, he noted, spent millions on the June 2 primary and the task of gearing up the machinery for a second primary would be not only extravagantly costly but would defeat the whole primary system because few voters would be sufficiently informed to take part in a second go-around this year [1964].

Mahoney acknowledged, however, that if the Democrats should win control of one or both houses of the legislature next Nov. 3 under the present apportionment system, the Republican majority would be tempted to call a post-election special session to salvage as many seats as possible.

At radio station WMCA the mood was one of celebration and determination. President R. Peter Straus proudly exclaimed:

The decision is a knockout. The decision smashes the notion that there are different classes of voters, lightweights and heavyweights.

Now New Yorkers from Niagara to Nassau will be fairly and equally represented in state government, with one vote for one man in both houses in Albany. Now fourteen million of us in cities and suburbs reaching 500 miles from the Alleghenies to the St. Lawrence can begin looking to Albany for championship government.

Meanwhile, there was considerable activity taking place in the law offices of WMCA's legal counsel, Leonard Sand. The Supreme Court, as will be recalled, had limited its decision to the act of striking down New York's apportionment. It had not stated when or how the District Court should implement the ruling. On June 17, Sand, Straus, attorneys for the City of New York and Nassau County, William Boyd of the National Municipal League, David Wells of the International Ladies' Garment Workers' Union, and Dean Robert McKay met to consider whether to press for an immediate reapportionment despite the obvious dislocation of time schedules, primaries, etc. The alternative was to agree that no action need be taken until after the 1964 election, but to insist that it be taken immediately thereafter. The consensus was that the language of the Supreme Court gave a basis for asking for immediate action, although the fact situation in New York made the chances for success dubious. On June 29, the New York *Times* noted in an editorial:

> Under the Supreme Court's decision that both houses of a bicameral state legislature must be apportioned on the basis of population, the whole legislative structure of New York State—and most of the other states as well—will have to be redesigned and rebuilt.
>
> Many proposals have already been advanced for dealing with the problem—so many, in fact, that it would clearly be desirable to establish a bipartisan commission, with an expert technical staff, to begin evaluating the entire situation and preparing recommendations for a system consistent with the court's ruling. This would reduce or eliminate the temptation to gerrymander districts, which any legislature finds it practically impossible to resist.
>
> Without a commission in New York, the whole matter could get so bogged down in partisan strife that the Federal District Court might feel impelled to take the matter into its own hands. This has happened in a few states, but the courts have neither the experience nor the technical staffs to make them the ideal instrument for drawing district lines.

That same day, Governor Rockefeller announced that he would appoint a special committee of "outstanding" citizens "to undertake a prompt and objective study of the profound and historic questions

concerning the structure of representative government in the legislative branch raised by the Supreme Court's decisions." Moreover,
he promised that as soon as the committee gave him its report, he
would call a special session of the legislature to draft and enact an
apportionment plan.

The July 1 New York *Times* complimented the Governor's decision in an editorial entitled, "One Person, One Vote—When?":

> Governor Rockefeller is taking the sound first step toward meeting
> the Supreme Court's prescription for a reapportionment of the New
> York Legislature. He will name a special bipartisan committee to
> study the "profound and historic questions" raised by the Court and
> give him guidance in calling a special session of the legislature this
> year to act on the mandate for a legislature based on population.
>
> The primary question is, of course, whether it is feasible to enact
> a redistricting that would apply to the election of all members of the
> legislature this November. The answer is probably no, when all ele-
> ments of a tight political calendar are considered.

On July 11, Judge Sylvester J. Ryan set July 15 as the date for
hearings on the implementation decree which was to be issued in accordance with the Supreme Court's mandate. The following day,
Governor Rockefeller announced the appointment of a seven-mem-
ber Citizen's Committee on Reapportionment. William H. Mulligan,
dean of the Fordham University Law School was named chairman,
and his six colleagues on the committee were Joseph P. Craugh, an
upstate insurance executive, Charles R. Diebold, a Buffalo banker,
Roswell L. Gilpatric, a New York City lawyer and former deputy
secretary of defense in the Kennedy-Johnson administration, Judge
Francis E. Rivers, formerly of the Civil Court of the City of New
York, and George M. Shapiro and Eli Whitney Debevoise, New York
City attorneys.

The committee was to consider ten questions:

1. Whether a new apportionment plan should be embodied in a
constitutional amendment or in a statute.
2. Whether a constitutional convention should be convened to
consider a new apportionment plan.

3. How "population" should be measured and whether a new census should be taken to reflect the latest figures.

4. Whether the terms of legislators should continue to be two years, or whether longer terms are now desirable.

5. Whether the number of members of either or both houses of the legislature should now be changed or whether any other change in the structure of the legislature should be made.

6. Whether district lines should be drawn exclusively by the legislature, or by some other body, or remain a shared responsibility between the legislature and local legislative bodies as at present.

7. What significance should be attached to political subdivisions in an apportionment plan.

8. Whether the vote of individual legislators should be weighted according to population.

9. Whether reapportionments should be required more or less frequently than once every ten years.

10. Whether changes in the election law and the state's election machinery are necessary in connection with a new apportionment plan.

On July 15, the hearing on the implementation decree took place in the District Court before Circuit Judge Sterry R. Waterman and District Judges Sylvester J. Ryan and Richard H. Levet, the same three judges who had heard WMCA's case the two previous times it had been argued in the District Court.

Samuel A. Hirshowitz, first assistant attorney general, representing the state began by presenting his argument succinctly:

> Your Honor, summing up in advance our position, our position is that the election of 1964 should be held in accordance with present existing constitutional and statutory provisions, upon the ground that it would be inequitable to change the rules at this particular point in the course of the election year.

Following this brief statement, however, Hirshowitz spoke at great length on such diverse topics as the reaction of the Washington bar to the Supreme Court's decisions, the dissatisfaction expressed at the convention of the National Association of Attorneys General and the unfairness of WMCA's allegation that the Governor was stalling on reapportioning the state. At this point, Judge Waterman lost his patience and remarked sharply: "I take it, Mr. Hirshowitz, all that you are telling us you told us in the first sentence, which was that the state takes the position that the elections should go along, as originally said."

Undaunted, Hirshowitz continued in his discursive manner, addressing himself to everything except the question Judge Waterman had put to him, namely, what arguments could the state set forth to justify its position that the fall election should take place as scheduled under New York's unconstitutional apportionment?

Noting tersely that "we read the New York *Times,*" Judge Waterman tried in vain to pin Hirshowitz down on when the state planned to reapportion, whether the state believed that reapportionment could be carried by legislative act or only by constitutional amendment and whether the state thought that only the apportionment formula proper had been struck down by the Court or whether collateral constitutional provisions had been invalidated as well. At last, after a long discussion about the practical political problems an early reapportionment would cause, Waterman asked in despair, "Does anyone else have any suggestions?" At that point, Leonard Sand began his argument for WMCA.

Sand's position was that "in the first instance the legislature [ought to] be given the opportunity" to draw up new district lines, but that the Court should also enjoin any election pursuant to the invalidated formula and make clear that if the state fails to act—"and it has given the indication to date that it will"—the Court itself will take action. He also offered, in the event that the legislature took no action, to present his own apportionment plan.

After refusing to allow Hirshowitz to speak, Judge Waterman heard Professor Jack B. Weinstein, Nassau County attorney. Weinstein argued that the question of whether the Court should demand immediate apportionment must be considered in terms of the relative equities of each side.

> *Mr. Weinstein:* On the one hand, you have the individual constitutional rights of literally millions of people of the state who have

for years been denied those rights, who are denied those rights today, and who now, it is suggested, ought to be denied those rights for
at least two years in the future.

•   •   •

Now, on the other hand, what do you have? . . . First, that there
is the right in the status quo, the preservation of the status quo. It
seems to me, that equity is clearly out; it need be given no weight at
all and no consideration.

Second, that a number of individuals in this state have spent considerable time and money in primary campaigns and in election ex-
penses of one kind or another and that those expenditures would be
wasted.

•   •   •

The fact that something was done on the basis of an unconstitutional system and money was spent provides no basis, really, for continuing that system. So this argument about primaries seems of no
weight at all.

Third, that it's costly to act now. The costs involved here will have
to be expended in any event. Money will have to be spent to draw
maps. People are going to have to sit down and work through the
night to draw up a plan. The question of spending it now or spending
it in two years is really of no great significance.

After a recess, Judge Waterman announced:

We think we have arrived at a proper resolution as of today, and
this is our unanimous order:

The Court declares and adjudges the present scheme of legislative
apportionment of the State of New York to be unconstitutional and
void, and the Court recesses until Friday, July 24, at 10:30 A.M., to
await action, if any, by the duly constituted authorities of the State
of New York in the light of this declaration, and to hear any further
representations by the parties litigant toward further implementation
of the judgment of the Court.

Later that same afternoon Sand sent a telegram to the Attorney
General's office requesting permission to inspect and copy informa-

tion, data, statistics, and maps in the possession of the Joint Legislative Committee on Reapportionment in order that WMCA might
meet the Court's request for submitting a reapportionment plan.
The following morning Sand was advised that the committee would
not make the information available to him. He immediately went
before Judge Ryan—Judges Waterman and Levet were not in the
city at the time—to ask for a court order to the committee to produce
the requested material.

Judge Ryan opened the hearing by noting, as he would several
times in the course of the afternoon, that his "reaction would be that
it might be most desirable and most helpful that the Legislative Committee would make these [materials] available without an order of
the Court." The state, however, refused to comply.

First Assistant Attorney General Hirshowitz insisted that the Attorney General's office had no objection, but that he did not represent
the committee and feared political repercussions if he interfered with
the legislature's domain. Ryan, unimpressed by Hirshowitz's objections, announced that he would issue a subpoena requiring that the
materials be produced in Court.

Then occurred one of the most bizarre incidents of the entire five-
year controversy. R. Peter Straus, fearful of the possible removal or
destruction of documents between the Friday (July 17) on which
Judge Ryan said he would issue the subpoena and the following
Wednesday when it would be returnable, decided, despite Sand's
strong opposition, to hire and station a Pinkerton detective outside
the Joint Legislative Committee offices to guard the records. A de-
scription of what transpired that evening in Albany is contained in
an article in the Albany *Times Union* of July 17, written by Doc
Rivett.

GUARD WATCHES GUARD GUARDING CAPITOL
A Long Day's Hassle; A Final Compromise

Herbert Faurote, a sergeant in the Pinkerton protective service,
sat in a straight-backed cushioned chair last night in a fourth-floor
corridor of the Capitol—a living monument to the perseverance and
sense of history of R. Peter Straus.

Sergeant Faurote, a tall, thin, slightly stooped man armed with a

badge No. 23 and a slim plastic portfolio, was watching the entrance
to the three-office suite of the Joint Legislative Committee on Reapportionment.

He was the first private cop in anyone's memory to sit as a watchman over a legislative committee. A Capitol guard sat with him. He
was watching the watchman.

Mr. Faurote is watching at long distance over maps, charts and
documents of the committee, which are under subpoena to be produced in Federal Court in New York next Tuesday morning.

They are vital, Mr. Straus said, to a three-judge Federal Court's
ruling on when and how New York must set up a new districting
plan.

Mr. Straus, a slim, young-looking radio executive, hired Mr.
Faurote—and successive Pinkerton men every eight hours—at the
end of a day of court action and harsh accusations.

But it took three hours to make sure that the watchman could
watch. In the process, several echelons of state government were
shaken.

•   •   •

. . . Mr. Straus, vacationing in Saranac Lake, flew his own plane
to Albany to take up the fight. He was met by three aides and Sergeant Faurote and they all went to the fourth floor to watch the
committee's doors. That was about 5 P.M.

Just before 6, Alfred H. Hallenbeck, the building superintendent,
asked them to leave the floor. So everyone went to his first floor office, to be joined by five reporters, two photographers and a television
crew.

Mr. Hallenbeck didn't want to say no, but he couldn't say yes to
having an outsider in the Capitol all night.

He made some calls for advice. Then he had Mr. Straus phone
Col. G. S. Smith, director of the division of real property management in the Office of General Services.

•   •   •

A half-hour later, Colonel Smith walked into the office.

"Now would you give me the details again," he said. "Got a couple
of busted eardrums in the war and don't hear so well on the phone."

"Three . . . years . . . ago . . . a group . . . of citizens," Mr.
Straus repeated.

When he was through, Colonel Smith said: "I can't make a decision on this; I just wanted to get the facts straight."

So he called Robert D. Stone, deputy commissioner of the Office of General Services. And Mr. Straus began again: "Three years ago, a group of citizens. . . ." Fortunately, Mr. Stone was familiar with the case and reporters were spared still another rendition.

"I'll have to talk to some people," Mr. Stone advised Mr. Straus.

A little under an hour later, Mr. Stone walked in and said: We're perfectly prepared to let you have someone on the fourth floor and we'll have one of ours."

On the fourth floor, a slight contretemps developed when Mr. Stone learned the watchman would be there till Tuesday.

"Well, that's a long time," he said, and suggested only two shifts till 9 A.M. Mr. Straus, by now ready to compromise, suggested: "Can't we agree that he can stay here until we talk further?" "All right," said Mr. Stone, "until the subpoena is returned or other arrangements are made."—Rivett.

The following day, Friday, July 17, Assistant Attorney General Hirshowitz appeared before Judge Ryan, who was later joined by Judge Levet, and informed him that the committee would make the materials available to the plaintiffs. Thereupon Judge Ryan agreed not to issue the subpoena and warned all parties that he didn't want any "unseemly conflicts" to take place when attorneys and workers for WMCA appeared at the committee's offices to copy the needed information.

Sand recalled:

On July 20, we went to the offices of the Joint Legislative Committee on Reapportionment in the State Capitol Building. Everything about these offices is unique. For example, they are located on a mezzanine between the fourth and fifth floor of the Capitol. A sign on the door states, accurately enough, "This is not the fourth floor. This is not the fifth floor."

But the most unique aspect of these offices is the secrecy in which they are shrouded. The Democratic Minority Leader of the Senate, Joseph Zaretzki, was later to ask me with amazement whether I was really granted access to the committee's map room. "They won't let me in," he complained.

We were accompanied to the committee offices by George H. P. Dwight and Joel Cohen of the Corporation Counsel's office and Benjamin Klapper and William D. Siegel of the Nassau County Attorney's office. Our escort was State Senator Robert C. McEwen, chairman of the committee, and then a candidate for Congress [he was elected in November, 1964].

The first condition which Senator McEwen imposed was that the press be present during our examination of the records, despite Judge Ryan's admonition concerning publicity. As a result, members of the Capitol press staff would wander in and out while we were marking the documents which we wanted photostated. When the press was present, there was a tendency to make speeches. In view of Senator McEwen's candidacy for Congress and the fact that some upstate counties had then just endorsed Peter Straus to be the Democratic candidate for the United States Senate [Robert F. Kennedy was subsequently nominated and then went on to defeat Senator Kenneth Keating in the November election], this was easy enough to understand.

The huge maps which were in the committee's offices were too large to photostat and the committee would not let us take them back to New York where a hurriedly assembled group of volunteers was waiting to work on them. We did obtain and photostat the citizen census figures which were our primary need and from that evening until the July 27 hearing, the volunteers worked literally around the clock to prepare the proposed apportionment.

Precisely at 10 o'clock on the morning of July 27, 1964, Judges Sterry R. Waterman, Sylvester J. Ryan and Richard H. Levet began hearings on the form implementation of the Supreme Court's decision should take.

Attorney General Louis Lefkowitz assured the Court that the state was proceeding to effectuate the Court's order as quickly as possible, but that the complexity of apportionment was so great that a new plan could not possibly be put into effect until the 1966 general election. "The best interests of the people of the state," Lefkowitz urged, "require that this matter be given not hasty consideration, more than cursory consideration, but mature consideration." Such consideration was currently being given the matter by Dean Mulligan's Citizen's Committee on Reapportionment.

Judge Levet seemed unimpressed by the necessity of waiting for Mulligan's report. He thought that most of the questions the committee were considering were irrelevant so far as apportionment was concerned. The immediate issue before the Court, Levet stated, was whether or not the state could apportion before the November, 1964, election.

To this Lefkowitz replied that a new apportionment "would cause a disruption of an election already in progress, of a primary that has taken place," and make demands which, under current provisions of the election law, would be physically impossible to meet.

Since the state refused to act before the coming election, the question Judge Ryan raised was "whether or not this Court should take judicial action which would affect the election and the candidates . . . in the coming November election." Lefkowitz responded by assuring the Court that apportionment "is a legislative function."

Judge Levet then asked:

> Suppose we made it a condition that a new term be enacted and set up for the year 1966. In other words, whatever is done here, whatever deferral is granted, is an act of grace. If one of the conditions of grace is that there be a new plan for the year 1966 and a special election be held for one year or for three years or for whatever term it may be, in other words, so that the term of the 1964 electees is limited to 1965, what is wrong with it?

Although Lefkowitz insisted that such an election would fly "in the face of a constitutional provision that calls for a two-year term," Judge Waterman thought that "that doesn't make any difference." Judge Ryan, however, thought otherwise:

> *I don't think that this Court has any power to amend the state constitution by its judicial act. I think the Supreme Court has held certain provisions of our state constitution remains intact. This Court has no power by a judicial act to accomplish an amendment of the state constitution.**

* Author's italics.

The following exchange then took place:

> *Judge Waterman:* Suppose we let this election go on subject to [the] injunction . . . that the legislature do nothing else except pass a reapportionment measure[?]
>
> *Judge Levet:* That would hold up all other business of the legislature.
>
> *Judge Waterman:* Including the budget, the levying of taxes, the payment of state employees, et cetera.
>
> *Mr. Lefkowitz:* I can only say that in a state like New York, with the budget having been adopted and to go into effect in the fiscal period beginning April first, and many of the towns and counties relying on the action of the legislature, you would have a pretty chaotic condition.
>
> *Judge Waterman:* If there is a choice of chaotic conditions between granting the plaintiffs' order and that, which is better?

>   •   •   •

> *Judge Ryan:* Let me ask you one question, if I may: What is the objection to having this election proceed as scheduled in the assembly districts and senatorial districts as presently laid out and providing for a weighted vote for those elected to office? What would be the valid objection to that?

Lefkowitz's response was: The state constitution forbade it.

Sand, in a biting opening address, accused the state of taking advantage of the election situation to further the aims of the Republican party:

> The state has said that there are profound questions and that they cannot act until they get resolved, but on December first [the date the Mulligan Report was due] the clouds part and the sun comes through and the profound questions are all resolved just in time to permit a lame duck legislature to sit and pass on a new apportionment.
>
> What is the significance of the December first date as opposed to January first except to permit lame-duck action?

Since the legislature refused to take action, the Court must itself afford plaintiffs' relief, Sand argued.

We don't urge weighted voting as a permanent solution. We are supremely mindful of its disadvantages and to some extent of its repugnance to our traditional notions of how a legislature should function, but as an interim measure to be adopted only in the event of the legislature not taking other action prior to its effective date it absolutely eliminates all mechanical, political, practical difficulties with which the state's papers are so filled.

Professor Weinstein, Nassau County attorney, presented the Court with the apportionment plan he had earlier promised that his office would produce. An amusing interchange then took place as Weinstein pointed out that, in his opinion, there was only one obstacle that stood in the way of the Court's adopting his plan.

Mr. Weinstein: The central difficulty here, if I may respectfully suggest it, is the difficulty imposed by judicial inhibition—
Judge Levet: What, sir?
Mr. Weinstein:—judicial inhibition in this area.
Judge Waterman: Self-restraint. I think every lawyer is acquainted with my two associates and knows that neither of them has an inhibition.
Mr. Weinstein: I am not speaking in any psychoanalytic sense.
Judge Ryan: It is essential in this circuit that district judges have no inhibitions.

Professor Weinstein then went on to explain, at greater length, precisely what he meant by "judicial inhibitions."

I am talking about the entirely proper and sound constitutional reluctance of the federal judiciary to compel the highest officials of a state to take action they do not wish to take and to particularly take action in a field as sensitive and delicate politically as this, a field which strikes directly at the state's most intimate political processes. And that really seems to us to be the gist of the difficulty.

. . .

Now there are, we recognize, these very strong self-imposed barriers. As Judge Cardozo said, in *The Nature of the Judicial Process,* there are the limits of nature and custom and the almost undefinable practice which other judges have set, which are too hard and difficult for judges to overcome. But the Court can have no alternative but to overcome those inhibitions in this case.

After a three-hour recess, the Court reconvened to announce its implementation order.* By unanimous consent, Judge Waterman ordered that:

> Inasmuch as the primary elections of June 2, 1964, had been held and nominees chosen prior to the decision of the Supreme Court of June 15, 1964, and in view of the imminence of the 1964 election of members of the New York State Legislature and in order to give the New York State Legislature an opportunity to fashion a constitutionally valid legislative apportionment plan, *the 1964 election of Assemblymen and Senators shall be conducted as presently scheduled; provided that the terms of said members so elected on November 3, 1964, or at any special election to fill vacancies, shall expire on December 31, 1965, the legislature shall have enacted into law a valid apportionment scheme that is in compliance with the XIV Amendment of the United States Constitution and which shall be implemented so as to effect the election of members of the legislature at the election in November, 1965. Members so elected to hold office for a term of one year ending December 31, 1966.*†

* This decision was upheld by the Supreme Court on February 1, 1965 by a per curiam opinion in *Hughes* v. *WMCA*.

† Author's italics.

11

New York Reapportions
Its Legislature

R. W. Apple, Jr., reporting on the District Court's implementation decree in the July 28 edition of the New York *Times,* commented that the decision "was a defeat for the Democrats, who had asked the Court to order immediate redistricting." He continued: "However, it was not an unqualified victory for the Republicans, who had hoped the Court would give them two more years in which to reapportion."

"Sources in Albany," Apple related, "reported that Governor Rockefeller was almost certain to call a special session in December to enact a reapportionment bill." The reason for this, according to Apple, was that "many Republicans believe that the legislature to be elected in November this year will be less strongly controlled by their party than the present one." By passing a reapportionment bill before January 1, the Republicans could insure that the new apportionment would favor their party's interests.

State Senate Majority Leader Walter J. Mahoney, a Republican, commented that he was "grateful that the Court has refused to be rushed into precipitate action by the intemperate and self-serving demand of the New York City Democratic bosses."

Mayor Robert Wagner of New York City, however, praised the decision, declaring:

> We in the city can only be pleased at the decision of the Federal Court. The cause of fair apportionment has been advanced.
> We must be ever vigilant to assure that the plan and the districting

are fair in every respect and to frustrate the efforts that are almost certain to be made to gerrymander the districts for partisan advantage.

The Adirondack *Daily Enterprise,* an upstate New York newspaper, praised the decision in an editorial on July 29 and blamed the state's political leaders for the fact that the Court had to take any action at all.

STEP TOWARD REAPPORTIONMENT

The three-man court ruling on reapportionment is a compromise which seems to have made both sides happy. The decision was that the elections would go forward normally this year, but there would be special elections for the reapportioned districts next year. For assemblymen, this will mean three elections in as many years.

This procedure will be hard on the assemblymen, but it is better they put up with a little hardship than the present system continue.

There were many chances to change the districts before and our own State Senator, Robert C. McEwen, headed the committee to do the job. But this committee was more interested in keeping its own party in power than in creating the fairest possible districts.

In the case of New York State, the party wanting to stay in power by this means happened to be the Republicans; in other states, Democrats have done the same thing for the same reason.

•   •   •

The matter was forced into the Court's hands because the politicians refused to put responsibility above self-interest, and now they must abide by the rulings of the Court.

On August 4, Assembly Speaker Joseph F. Carlino proposed that the membership of the Assembly be increased from its present total of 150 seats to make possible an apportionment system that would enable each of the state's sixty-two counties to have its own representative and yet would not violate the Court's one man, one vote edict. He also suggested that weighting the vote of the legislators in accordance with the number of people they represented might be a simple and effective way to comply with the Supreme Court's ruling.

A month later, Ronald Sullivan of the New York *Times* reported that Carlino was predicting a "virtual legislative stalemate" as a result of the Federal Court's implementation order. "Legislators normally are reluctant to vote new taxes," the speaker said. "When they do, it's always in the first session, not the year when they're up for re-election." He pointed out that if the Assembly remained at 150 members, fifteen to eighteen incumbents, most of them Republicans, would lose their seats to areas with larger populations. "It would be very difficult to get these men to vote for new revenues," Carlino commented.

Carlino's dire predictions evoked a heated response from the New York *World Telegram and Sun*. In a September 9 editorial, entitled, "Oh, Those Hurdles," the paper took New York politicians to task:

> Oh, the hurdles that honest reapportionment faces in this state are something to contemplate.
>
> There are some who think districting on the basis of equal population, as mandated by the Supreme Court, is odious and outrageous per se. . . . And there are those who regard reapportionment as a hobbling nuisance.
>
> Consider the forecast of Assembly Speaker Joseph F. Carlino. He envisions a "stalemate" in Albany next year because, by court order, legislators elected this year will have one-year terms. So will legislators elected next year under reapportionment. Biennial elections are to resume in 1966.
>
> This, coupled with a prospective budget crisis, is going to make it tough on the lawgivers elected this year, according to Carlino.
>
> Quote: "Legislators normally are reluctant to vote new taxes. When they do, it's always in the first session, not the year when they're up for re-election."
>
> There, for free, is a lesson (of sorts) in statesmanship.
>
> No wonder various state politicians hope to upset the reapportionment timetable. Heaven forfend that they should have to endure the pitfalls of two consecutive election years!

On October 19, a spokesman for Governor Rockefeller announced that a special session of the legislature would be called for early December to enact a new apportionment for New York State. State

Democratic Chairman William H. McKeon angrily called on Democratic members of the legislature to boycott the special session. Expressing confidence that Democrats would gain control of the legislature in the November 3 election, McKeon said that any lame-duck session controlled by the Republicans would be "an insult and disservice to the people of the state."

Governor Rockefeller, in reply, called McKeon's proposal "a cynical and politically motivated call for a mass violation of law by elected officials," and voiced confidence that "no Senator or Assemblyman will violate his oath of office and his constitutional responsibilities by participating in such a boycott."

The New York *Times,* in a biting editorial, called Rockefeller's motives "suspect."

> . . . [T]he only discernible reason for putting a lame-duck legislature in charge of the reapportionment is desperate haste to salvage any Republican advantage that can be gained in redrafting district lines. A month later, in early January, a new legislature to be elected on Nov. 3 will convene. This is the one that, bearing the most recent political mandate from the voters, ought to have jurisdiction over reapportionment.

Nor did the *Times* appreciate McKeon's antics. In the same editorial, it noted:

> Democratic State Chairman McKeon has come up with an utterly irresponsible proposal. . . . [His] is a lawless approach to lawmaking, a call for insubordination against the legislator's oath of office. Mr. McKeon does his party's candidates for the legislature a poor service by the example he has set in irresponsibility.

A few days later, twenty-eight of the state's leading Democratic legislators, headed by Senate Minority Leader Joseph Zaretzki and Assembly Minority Leader Anthony J. Travia, warned Governor Rockefeller that redistricting by a "lame-duck legislature" would "raise the gravest constitutional and legal questions."

Noting that "the participation of legislators of either party who have just been defeated at the polls and the affront to their constituents and to their party who will take office a few weeks later cannot create a favorable climate for a constructive, nonpartisan effort to comply with the edict of the federal courts," the Democrats called upon the Governor "to announce immediately that he will put the apportionment question in the hands of the legislature which the people will elect in November." The statement continued: "For the Governor to ram this issue through such a last-minute session would be an outrageous and contemptible effort to buy political casualty insurance at the expense of the people of New York."

On November 3, 1964, Lyndon Baines Johnson was elected President by an overwhelming majority. He carried forty-four states and the District of Columbia with 61% of the popular vote and a record 15,529,886 plurality. Senator Barry Goldwater, the defeated Republican candidate, received only 52 electoral votes, taking, in addition to his home state of Arizona, five Southern states—Alabama, Georgia, Louisiana, Mississippi and South Carolina.

In New York State, Johnson scored a record sweep, carrying all sixty-two counties. The first Democrat to win in Westchester and Nassau since 1912 and the first to take Suffolk in modern history, his margin in the state was better than 2 to 1.

The effect of Goldwater's candidacy upon New York Republicans was nothing short of disastrous. Senator Kenneth Keating, who was defeated by Robert F. Kennedy, ran 1.8 million votes ahead of Goldwater. Swept along on Johnson's coattails the Democrats won New York's congressional delegation by a 28-13 margin.

The results in state elections were even more momentous. The Democrats won control of both houses of New York's legislature for the first time since 1935. Speaker Carlino and Senate Majority Leader Mahoney both were defeated. The new legislature was to be composed of thirty-four Democrats and twenty-four Republicans in the Senate, and eighty-eight Democrats and sixty-two Republicans in the Assembly.

After the Republican's catastrophic defeat in the state elections, Governor Rockefeller's insistence upon calling a special session of the legislature to reapportion the State was, the New York *Times* noted, "a travesty on the democratic process."

The *Times'* own faith in "the democratic process" also seemed somewhat diminished. In a searing editorial the paper exclaimed:

> There is every reason to suspect the Republican leaders of an effort to draft a reapportionment as favorable to their party as they can get away with. There is equal reason to expect the Democratic party, if it does the job in the regular legislative session starting Jan. 6, to favor itself to the same limit. What the public wants, however, is scrupulously fair reapportionment, without discrimination, without gerrymander. We doubt that either party is capable of such high-mindedness.
>
> A far better guarantee of fairness from the beginning in the drafting of new maps would be to put the job in the hands of a nonpartisan commission, or a bipartisan one, while there is still time to do so. Then the public would have some confidence in the finished product.
>
> Governor Rockefeller is understandably eager to rebuild a bruised and beaten Republican party. Calling a lame-duck session on reapportionment would give the party just one more black eye in a very bad 1964.

The same day, November 6, Senator Zaretzki warned that the Democrats intended to scrap any "gerrymandered" legislative reapportionment that the Republicans might enact at a special session of the lame-duck legislature. The Democrats, he asserted, would pass their own plan when they gained control of the legislature in January. Moreover, he stated, if Rockefeller vetoed the Democratic plan, he would put the rural apportionments before the three-judge Federal Court.

On November 30, the long-awaited Mulligan Report was released. The Citizens Committee on Reapportionment recommended that: (1) the State redistrict by statute rather than constitutional amendment; (2) the term of Senate members be increased to four years and the term of Assembly members be kept to two years; (3) bicameralism be continued; (4) the number of legislators in both the Assembly and Senate be increased; (5) county lines be observed wherever possible; (6) fractional, rather than weighted, voting be considered;* (7) reapportionment take place every ten years; and (8) changes be made in both the state's election law and machinery.

R. W. Apple, Jr., writing in the December 1 New York *Times* commented that reaction to the Mulligan Report "developed quickly and along predictable lines—praise from Republicans, criticism from Democrats." Governor Rockefeller allegedly told reporters, "I don't care if the Democrats don't like it [enacting a new apportionment during a special session]." However, a spokesman from his office later said that the Governor's actual statement was: "If the Democrats were in my position, they would do the same thing."

As predicted, on December 1, Governor Rockefeller called for a special session of the legislature to meet December 15. "The public importance of reapportionment," Rockefeller declared, "requires that it be considered at a special session, at which the legislature can act unburdened by the weight of other important public matters."

The next day it was reported that fractional voting would be employed in the Republicans' apportionment plan. Senate Minority Leader Zaretzki immediately replied that the adoption of fractional voting would be fought by the Democrats on the floor of the legislature and in the courts. "If they go for fractional voting," Zaretzki warned, "we will take that as proof of a partisan hatchet job. Fractional voting obviously doesn't fall within the confines of the Supreme Court's decision." "According to my information," the legislator continued, "they plan to give these people [representatives] fractional votes on roll calls, but full votes on organizing the Assembly and full votes in committees. Obviously, that won't wash with what the Court had in mind."

Straus, in a biting editorial, castigated the Republicans for the secrecy with which they were proceeding to draw up their new apportionment scheme:

* Under a system of fractional voting, no legislator would have more than a single vote but those legislators who represented districts containing fewer people than the state-wide average would be given a fractional vote— possibly as little as one-sixth of a vote—proportionate to the size of the electorate they represent. In contrast, under a system of weighted voting, no legislator would receive less than a full vote but those legislators who represented districts containing more people than the state-wide average would be given a multiple of votes proportional to the size of the electorate they represent.

Three top Republican leaders and a man from Governor Rockefeller's office have met every day this past week with local Republicans
in Batavia, Auburn, Utica, Glen Falls, Albany, Newburgh and New
York City to review a secret reapportionment plan.

The apparent GOP strategy is to keep the plan away from the
public until December 15 when the special session of the lame-duck
legislature is scheduled to meet and rubber stamp the secret Republican plan without any public scrutiny.

New York State shouldn't be divided in the dark. WMCA calls
on the Governor to release his reapportionment plan to the public
now. The public has a right to know.

Layhmond Robinson reported in the December 6 New York
Times, "Mr. Carlino would not say what decision had been made on
the size of the two legislative houses, but it was learned from other
sources that the Assembly would be increased from its present
strength of 150 members to between 165 and 180 members. . . . It
was also learned that the Republican legislative leaders expected to
increase the number of Senators from 58, as at present, to 65, a figure
recommended by the citizens committee."

The Republican leaders, Robinson continued, insisted that the
reapportionment plan they would enact at the special session would
be "fair and equitable." While it would increase the representation of
the populous urban and suburban areas, the Republicans noted, it
would also "assure each of the smaller counties an effective legislative
voice." Disclaiming any attempt to achieve partisan advantage, the
leaders pointed out that "any plan, whether it be enacted by a Republican or Democratic legislature, must be approved by the federal
courts before it becomes operative."

Republican assurances failed to convince the New York *Times.*
In a December 8 editorial, the *Times* picked up Straus' argument
and denounced the Republicans for not letting the public know what
its apportionment plans were.

"SECRET" REAPPORTIONMENT

The Republican party leaders have been conferring privately with
county leaders and legislators throughout the state about their plans
for reapportioning the state legislature at the special session Governor

Rockefeller has summoned to meet a week from today. Now some of the proposals that have been discussed at these secret conclaves have come to light.

•   •   •

. . . [W]e strongly urge Governor Rockefeller to make the details of his plan public at once in order to give the citizens of this state an opportunity to study the plan and to form a balanced judgment on its merits. It will be recalled that when the Republicans redistricted the state's congressional districts in 1961 they then, too, withheld details until the very last moment—an action which this newspaper characterized as outrageous. Reapportionment is not solely the business of the Republican party; it is a matter in which the people of this state are vitally concerned, and about which they have every right to be fully informed before the fact.

The New York newspapers reported on December 11, 1964 that the Republicans intended to enact not one, but four apportionment plans. To accomplish this, the legislature would first pass "Plan A," the apportionment formula least advantageous to the Republican lawmakers. After it would be signed into law, a second plan, "Plan B," would be passed as an amendment to "Plan A." In the same way, "Plan C" would be passed as an amendment to "Plan B" and "Plan D," as an amendment to "Plan C." At the end of the process, Plan D, the one most conducive to the interests of the Republican party, would stand as state law.

The Court, commented R. W. Apple, Jr. of the New York *Times,* would, when it reviewed the state's apportionment, be able "to strip away the layers of law like leaves of an artichoke until it finds one that meets its standards of constitutionality."

"Officially," Apple noted, "Republican leaders explained their complicated strategy as a means of dealing with the varying interpretations of the precise meaning of the United States Supreme Court's one-man, one-vote decision of June 15. . . . In fact, as the more candid Republicans admit, the goal is to deny to the Democrats the opportunity to do the redistricting themselves."

Plan A would be based on citizen population and whole votes for each member of the legislature. Plan D, in contrast, would be based on the 1962 gubernatorial voting figures and would make use of fractional voting. Plans B and C would be variations of Plans A and D.

The advantage to the Republicans of using voting rather than citizen population figures was that a higher percentage of the residents in the Republican-controlled rural areas voted in the 1962 election than did the citizens in the Democratically-controlled urban areas. The disparity was, in fact, quite substantial. Only 29.4% of New York County's residents voted in that election as compared with the approximately 35% who voted in upstate Chemung County.

The Democrats, not to be outdone by their Republican rivals, offered two apportionment bills of their own. Announcing their plans, the Democrats charged:

> The special lame-duck session summoned by Governor Rockefeller was conceived in partisan disregard of the best interests of the people of this state. This partisan scheme is being carried forward in the face of outraged public opinion and editorial opposition.
>
> Our plan is designed to bring non-partisan order and equity out of a scheme for partisan gain.

The main feature of the Democratic plan was the provision for the creation of a bipartisan commission that would assume the responsibility of redistricting the legislature. The commission would contain eleven members, no more than five of whom could be legislators. The Senate majority and minority leaders and the Assembly majority and minority leaders would each appoint two members of the commission. The remaining three members would be selected by the Governor from a list of six nominees chosen by the presidents and chancellors of the six largest universities in the state—Columbia University, Cornell University, New York University, Syracuse University, the University of the City of New York, and the University of the State of New York. The nominees chosen by the Governor could not all be from the same party.

The commission, the Democratic leaders asserted, would insure that there was no more than a 15% population differential between the largest and smallest districts and that districts would wherever possible follow county lines and be as compact and contiguous as possible.

One of the Democratic bills called for a Senate of 60 members and an Assembly of 180; the other provided for a sixty-five-member Senate and a 195-member Assembly. In both plans each Senate district would be divided into three substantially equal Assembly districts and each legislator would have a single whole vote.

On December 17, additional details of the Republican apportionment bills were disclosed. Both Senate and Assembly lines would cross county and city lines.

Commenting on the G.O.P. reapportionment plan, the New York *Times* noted, with evident displeasure:

> The New York State leadership of the Republican party plans to put through the lame-duck legislature—assuming it is able to whip its balky or recalcitrant members into line—four reapportionment measures to fill the void created by the United States Supreme Court's one-man, one-vote ruling last June.
>
> Two provisions, both wide open to serious criticism, are embodied in the plan most favored by the Republicans. One is the use of voters as the measure of population, the other is the introduction of fractional voting in order to preserve the representation of small upstate counties by Assemblymen who would cast as little as one-sixth of a vote each.
>
> By providing that apportionment should be based on the 1962 gubernatorial vote, the Republicans are trying to write into law a flagrant partisan advantage. In that year New York City, which by the census of 1960 has 46.37 per cent of the state's population, cast only 41.91 per cent of the state's vote. There are arguments, even nonpartisan ones, that can be reasonably made for this procedure; but we feel that the countervailing arguments weigh more heavily.
>
> Many considerations affect the incidence of voting. It is well-established that areas where large numbers of people of low incomes and little education live do not cast votes proportionate to their numbers, yet these may be the people who most need legislative representation. Such haphazard occurrences as a violent storm may cut down voting in one district; a bitter local issue may bring out unusual numbers in another.

Unfortunately, the Supreme Court has not yet made it clear just
what it considers the proper basis for apportionment. In *Reynolds* v.
Sims Chief Justice Warren wrote that the overriding objective must be
substantial equality of population among the various districts, so that
the vote of any citizen is approximately equal in weight to that of any
other citizen in the state. He spoke of "citizens," "voters," "residents"
and "persons," almost interchangeably.

Until it was struck down by the Federal Court, the New York State
Constitution specified that apportionment should be based on citizens.
The National Municipal League recommends that population should
be the base. Citizens or residents . . . provide a more equitable basis
for apportioning legislative seats than the result of one election now
two years old.

· · ·

Fractional voting represents an attempt to preserve individual representation for the smaller counties upstate without making the Assembly
prohibitively large. Governor Rockefeller has defended it as the only
way in which they could retain an independent voice. The Republican
plan provides for an Assembly of 174 members with a total of 150
votes. Of these, 127 would be cast by members having one vote each,
and the remaining 23 would be shared by 47 individuals who would
have from one-sixth to three-quarters of a vote each.

Such a proposal clearly attempts to give special representation to
persons living in certain areas, and hence is of very dubious constitutionality. It is akin to the system of weighted voting that Chief
Justice Weintraub of New Jersey characterized as "absurd" when it
was argued before that state's highest court. A multi-county grouping
of smaller counties, such as is already envisaged for Senate districts,
would be far preferable.

Implicitly acknowledging the doubtful constitutionality of these
provisions, the Republicans propose to present their favored bill as
the last of the four to be enacted. The first plan would embody neither
the use of voters as a measure of population nor fractional voting; the
second would use voters as a base but be without fractional voting;
the third would contain fractional voting but omit the use of voters
as a measure. Then if the Federal Court strikes down the favored
Republican plan, the third will be on the statute books for its scrutiny.
If that should fail, the second and eventually the first would meet the
Court's gaze.

The one satisfying prediction that can be made with certainty is that the Federal Court will have the last word in this incredible procedure.

Layhmond Robinson of the New York *Times* wrote on December 21, "Democrats charged yesterday that Republicans were planning legislative districts shaped like turkeys, dragons and flying bats in an effort to double the number of seats in the Assembly and Senate held by New York City Republicans."

That same day the Republicans' problems were compounded when it was revealed that the Albany session on redistricting would be postponed again because the leaders had not yet completed work on their prospective measures. On December 23 and 24, however, the legislature finally managed to pass the four plans. By late Christmas Eve, the Governor had signed the last of them into law. The vote was strictly along party lines. The Republicans had met their deadline; they had passed the four reapportionment bills before losing control of the legislature.

12

New York Apportionment Acts and the Courts: Part I

Rockefeller and the Republican-controlled lame-duck legislature had won the apportionment battle in the political arena. Whether their victory would be sustained by the courts was another matter. Albin Krebs, in the New York *Herald Tribune,* reported that "the immediate challenge to the apportionment bills will come from Nassau County Attorney Jack B. Weinstein, who has been working feverishly over the Christmas weekend to draw up legal papers to submit to the three federal judges." On December 31, precisely one week after Governor Rockefeller signed Plan D into law, Weinstein filed a "Notice of Motion" in the District Court, asking the Court for an order invalidating the four apportionment acts on the grounds that: (1) the laws provided voting figures rather than citizen or resident figures; (2) the laws provided for fractional voting within the legislature; (3) "the laws provide[d] districts which are not compact and contiguous and depart in a substantial and unreasonable manner from natural geographic and political subdivision boundaries"; (4) the laws were adopted at a special session of the legislature; and (5) "the deliberate adoption of four separate and different laws to apportion and district at one session of the legislature with the intent to permit the judiciary to choose from among the four laws constituted an abdication of legislative responsibility to adopt a single law for apportionment and districting. . . ."

On January 4, Leonard Sand and WMCA joined Professor Weinstein in his challenge of the new apportionment. The following day R. Peter Straus explained to the public the reason for this latest litigation.

> One man, one vote. That's fair. But the voting power of a man in a rural county upstate was equal to eight Manhattan votes or twenty Nassau votes. That's unfair.
>
> So in 1961, WMCA asked the federal courts to make it fair by declaring that all votes must be equal in state elections. Three years later, the United States Supreme Court itself said we were right: You were being cheated outrageously in Albany.
>
> But then, Governor Rockefeller and a lame-duck Republican legislature pulled a fast one. They passed four different reapportionment laws, pretending to comply with the "one man, one vote" decision of the Supreme Court.
>
> The trouble is, each of the four laws continue to cheat city and suburban voters out of full and fair representation in Albany.
>
> WMCA is back in Federal Court and we are asking the Court to declare all four laws unconstitutional. A victory for WMCA will mean a victory for you and your voting rights.

In a publicity release issued the same day, Straus charged that the apportionment act gave "all of New York State an unhealthy dish of gerrymandering, or lame-duck pie." He also accused the legislature of using a "pie-slice technique to cut into the representation" of every metropolitan area in the state. "In Buffalo, Rochester, Syracuse, Albany and Greater New York," Straus explained, "you find the same slicing into metropolitan voting rights: A slim wedge of cities and suburbs, filled with voters, is attached to a wide chunk of rural territories, all crust."

Straus also announced that an experimental computerized districting of the city of Syracuse and the surrounding counties of Onondaga, Madison, and Oneida would be submitted to the Federal Court by WMCA. "We are going electronic," Straus said, "not because we think machines can draw sound districts for people, but simply to contrast the biased, gerrymandered lines drawn by the legislature with lines laid out by an impersonal non-political source."

The Syracuse region was selected, Straus pointed out, because:

"(1) it is essential to demonstrate that upstate cities and suburbs are as badly underrepresented, and worse, than New York City; (2) Greater Syracuse, at the geographical center of New York State, is typical of the more heavily populated metropolitan areas which have been gerrymandered by the legislature; and (3) in Greater Syracuse —as much as in any metropolitan region in the state—apportionment is already a live public issue whose significance is widely recognized and understood."

On Thursday, January 21, 1965, Judges Waterman, Ryan, and Levet began hearings on the challenge to New York's apportionment. Before listening to the attorneys, Judge Waterman issued a statement with which his colleagues concurred. After noting that wherever possible federal courts should abstain from interpreting state constitutions and laws, the judge noted that it was *"not the function of this Court to supervise the perimeters of districts, even though allegedly in violation of the New York State Constitution, if there are no invidious comparisons between the districts as to the populations or numbers of voters or numbers of citizens therein."** The districts did not display, Waterman continued, "any invidious discrimination relative to any person's race, color, creed, national origin or sex. . . ." The Constitution required the Court, Waterman asserted, only "to ascertain whether a vote for Assemblyman or Senator in one district is debased or diluted in relation to a vote for Assemblyman or Senator in another district, and to ascertain whether these districts are so constructed as to contain within them as nearly equal populations as is possible." "Hence," the judge concluded:

> . . . [A]ttacks upon the constitutional validity of these districts grounded upon alleged peculiarities of their shapes, alleged departures from claimed accustomed criteria for the fixing of electoral district perimeters and like allegations—in short, claimed legislative gerrymandering—we believe do not raise questions under the federal Constitution, and consequently we request of you that you devote none of your time in addressing us with reference thereto.

The Court's refusal to hear testimony on the question of whether New York's apportionment constituted gerrymandering clearly

* Author's italics.

stunned the lawyers for the plaintiffs, for they had planned to use the gerrymander issue as a major argument in their challenge of the Republican apportionment acts. Not surprisingly, Waterman drew laughter from the audience in the crowded courtroom when he noted that "some of you may be dissatisfied with this statement from the bench" and "some of you may have your arguments sort of maladjusted or reapportioned."

Orrin G. Judd, representing New York State, argued that the use of a voter base, rather than a citizen or resident base in apportioning seats was consistent with the demands of the Equal Protection Clause. He pointed out that under New York's apportionment system, "each vote shall have the same force and effect."

Fractional voting was justified by Judd on the grounds that it enabled the state to continue to recognize counties as the basic units of government. "Fractional voting," Judd noted, "has a considerable background in New York law. We have weighted voting in various branches of municipal government. The County of Nassau . . . has a system of weighted voting on its Board of Supervisors. . . . New York City has had a form of weighted voting in its Board of Estimates, and . . . in the New York Democratic County Executive Committee, everybody has fractional votes, varying from a half down to a sixth, and that is considered democratic, and I believe that the varied use of weighted and fractional voting successfully over a period of years shows that it is in conformity with sound principles of government, and there is nothing in the Constitution, the United States Constitution, which would require that it be set aside."

In answer to Judge Waterman's question of whether a special session of the legislature had the power to reapportion the state, Judd pointed out that "this Court having invalidated the Constitutional provisions governing reapportionment in New York, the requirement that legislation be enacted at a regular session would not affect it."

Leonard Sand began his argument by asserting that, as expressed by the Supreme Court: "State constitutional provisions should be deemed violative of the federal Constitution only when validly asserted constitutional rights could not otherwise be protected and effected. Clearly, courts should attempt to accommodate the relief ordered to the apportionment provisions of the state constitutions insofar as possible." The use of a voter base was therefore impermissible, Sand argued, because the state constitution provided for a citizen base. Fractional voting, Sand reasoned, was invalid because it required a double standard: One method of apportioning seats for densely populated counties and a different one for those in which fractional voting was to be employed.

After a fifteen-minute recess, Professor Weinstein began his argument for Nassau County. Weinstein pointed out that the major objections to the apportionment scheme were based on the assumption that the acts violated New York State's constitution. Since a challenge under state law had been filed in New York's own courts the previous day, proper federal-state relationships required the Federal District Court to defer action until the state court had an opportunity to decide the state questions.

Shortly before 5 p.m. on Tuesday, January 26, the Court handed down its decision: Plan A was held to comply with the implementation decree of July 27; Plans B, C and D were ruled invalid under the Fourteenth Amendment. The Court gave no reasons for its action but announced that an "explanatory" opinion would be filed shortly.

Reaction to the Court's decision was uniformly favorable, reported Ronald Sullivan in the January 27 New York *Times:*

> Republicans and Democrats alike declared here [Albany] tonight that a federal court's approval of a Republican plan for legislative reapportionment was a victory for their party.

· · ·

> Governor Rockefeller, expressing pleasure with the decision, said in a statement issued by his office here:
> "As I have said all along, our objective at the special session was to enact an apportionment law that would comply with the Supreme Court decision and the order of the Federal District Court, and I am pleased that the Court has so ruled.
> "As to the full scope and effort of the decision, no further comment is possible until the full opinions are handed down."

· · ·

However, a spokesman for William H. McKeon, Democratic state chairman, said the ruling merely opened the door to further Democratic attacks on the Republican plan. . . .

.   .   .

The man who originally challenged the constitutionality of New York's legislative apportionment, R. Peter Straus, president of radio station WMCA, said he looked forward to further court action.

In a statement issued in New York City, he said: "We are gratified that the Federal Court has upheld the principle of one-man, one-vote, striking down the most offensive evasions of that rule. We also are pleased that the Federal Court has retained jurisdiction, awaiting results of the fight that remains to be fought in the state court."

.   .   .

Justin Feldman, secretary of the New York County Democratic organization and a leader of the party's reapportionment drive, said tonight that he would ask the state's courts to rule the Republican plans invalid on the ground that they violated the state's constitution in several respects.

He said that according to the constitution, district lines must be "contiguous" and "compact."

However, he went on, the lines were gerrymandered under Plan A, towns were split, and the 150-member Assembly was altered. These were all, he said, in conflict with the state constitution.

.   .   .

Democratic legislative leaders said the decision would have no effect on plans to introduce their own formula, which calls for reapportionment by a non-partisan commission or a referendum.

In a thirty-two-page "explanatory" opinion filed on February 1, the District Court sought to bring order to an essentially chaotic situation. Judge Waterman, who emphasized that he was judging New York's apportionment exclusively under the provisions of the federal Constitution, generously noted that "under the unique circumstances of this case, it was not an abuse of our order for the legislature to enact four alternative plans rather than only one. At worst, insofar as the legislature's response to our order manifests its doubts about the validity of the plans which have been enacted, the presumption of constitutionality ordinarily accorded to legislation is weakened to some extent."

On the question of the validity of fractional voting, Judge Waterman's reasoning was more political than legal:

> If voting were the only important function of a legislator, the scheme of fractional voting in Plans D and C would probably not offend "the base standard of equality" among districts. But legislators have numerous important functions that have nothing directly to do with voting: participation in the work of legislative committees and party caucuses, debating on the floor of the legislature, discussing measures with other legislators and executive agencies, and the like. The Assemblyman who represents only one-sixth of a district can theoretically give each constituent six times as much representation in these respects as the Assemblyman who represents a full district. This disparity of representation persists even if the state is right in arguing that the Assemblyman with only one-sixth of a vote will carry only one-sixth as much political weight when he engages in these activities.

Plan A was valid, Waterman pointed out, because it created substantially equally populated districts:

> Under Plan A, the ratio of citizen populations between the largest and smallest districts in New York is 1.15:1 in the Senate and 1.21:1 in the Assembly, while the minimum percentage of citizens represented by a majority of the New York Legislature is 49.4% for the Senate and 49.3% for the Assembly. These minor deviations from perfect equality are clearly permissible under the federal Constitution.

"Of course," Judge Waterman noted, "the ultimate fitness of the scheme for their needs and purposes is for the people of the State of New York, themselves, to decide, and not for this Court to mandate."

13

New York Apportionment Acts and the Courts: Part II

While the Federal District Court was holding hearings on the validity, under the Fourteenth Amendment, of New York's four apportionment acts, another challenge to the Republican redistricting formulas was taking place in the New York State Supreme Court. On January 20, Jerome T. Orans, a Manhattan lawyer, obtained an order requiring Governor Rockefeller and other state officials to show cause why New York's new apportionment acts should not be declared in violation of the state constitution.

In the course of the lengthy hearings before Justice Levy that took place throughout the month of February, debate centered about the question of whether the United States Supreme Court, in its June decision in *WMCA* v. *Lomenzo,* had meant to invalidate all the provisions in the New York State Constitution which related to apportionment, or only those provisions which were clearly inconsistent with the Court's one-man, one-vote mandate.

Orrin Judd, special counsel for State Attorney General Louis Lefkowitz, argued that the effect of the Supreme Court's decision was to leave a gap in the apportionment provisions of New York State's Constitution—a gap which the legislature was free to fill in any way consistent with the requirements of the federal Constitution.

In marked contrast, Jerome Orans and the Village Independent Democrats, a reform club led by Edward I. Koch and Mrs. Carol Greitzer, maintained that state constitutional provisions setting a limit of 150 seats on the size of the Assembly and requiring that

town and county lines be observed and districts be compact and
contiguous still remain in full force.

Justice Levy, on March 15, handed down his ruling: He held all
four Republican reapportionment acts—Plans A, B, C and D—invalid under the New York State Constitution. In a meticulously
reasoned opinion, Levy considered the constitutional validity of: (1)
reapportionment at a special session of the legislature; (2) the legislative increase of the number of Assemblymen; (3) the 1964 reapportionment and redistricting of the state Senate; (4) gerrymandering
under the requirement of compact and contiguous districts; (5) division of county and town lines.

Levy found no constitutional flaw in passage of an apportionment
plan at a special session, but ruled the acts invalid on grounds that
they violated the state constitutional provision limiting the number of
Assemblymen to 150. Plan A, the only act left standing by the Federal District Court, had provided for an Assembly of 165.

Reaction to the merits of Justice Levy's opinion was generally
quite favorable. R. Peter Straus announced jubilantly:

> I'm absolutely delighted that the progress toward fair apportion-
> ment of the state is proceeding uninterrupted. The State Court has
> finished the housecleaning chore which the United States Supreme
> Court and the District Court began. The cobwebs of malapportion-
> ment have been wiped out.
>
> Now the legislature and the District Court are free to furnish the
> state with a modern, sensible apportionment and with clean, unpo-
> litical districts.

In an editorial entitled "New Start on Reapportionment," the New
York *Times* commented:

> The last of the cynical and politically oriented reapportionment
> measures passed by the lame-duck Republican legislature in December
> has now been swept from the statute books by court decision.
>
> Three of the four bills enacted were declared in violation of the
> federal Constitution by the special Federal Court having jurisdiction
> over reapportionment in this state. The fourth has now been declared
> in violation of the state constitution by Supreme Court Justice Mat-

thew M. Levy. His decision will undoubtedly be taken to the Court of Appeals.

New York State is now under a mandate from the Federal Court to enact a valid reapportionment law by April 1. It seems quite obvious now that this deadline cannot be met. While the Democrats controlling the legislature have announced that they intend to enact a reapportionment plan of their own, they have not yet even begun the complicated legislative processes of introducing and printing the necessary bills, holding public hearings and presenting the measures for debate in both houses. This procedure should not be carried out in crisis atmosphere.

By far the best course would be to create an independent bipartisan commission to take the drawing of district lines as far as possible out of the hands of the politicians and to place it in those of qualified experts. Perhaps that is too much to hope for, but the restraining influence of Governor Rockefeller's veto may yet keep the Democrats from the excesses that marred the Republican bills.

It is far more important that reapportionment be accomplished equitably than that it be rushed through to meet a deadline. For that reason, we welcome the announcement by radio station WMCA . . . that it will ask the Federal Court to modify the April 1 goal.

It may even turn out to be necessary to cancel the special election of a new legislature, next November, which had been ordered by the Federal Court, because even after the new district lines are drawn the permanent personal registration cards will have to be redistributed, a time-consuming process. This delay would be regrettable, but a lesser evil than too-hasty action.

New York is fortunate to have this second chance. The legislature must make better use of it than it did of its first opportunity.

In Albany, R. W. Apple, Jr. of the New York *Times* reported, "public comments by both Republicans and Democrats . . . were guarded." Governor Rockefeller announced that the state would appeal Levy's ruling, but failed to predict whether the November election could be held, saying, "this is a very difficult, delicate, complicated situation. The whole thing depends on the courts."

Rockefeller's great concern with the fate of New York's apportionment act before the courts was amply and quickly demonstrated:

On March 16, the day after Justice Levy's decision was handed down, it was announced that the state had engaged former Governor Thomas E. Dewey, the Republican presidential candidate in both 1944 and 1948 (he was defeated by Presidents Roosevelt and Truman, respectively), to argue its legislative apportionment litigation before the United States Supreme Court.

"Democrats Rage Over Dewey Job," reported Sydney H. Schanberg in the March 18 New York *Times*:

> Democratic legislators exploded in heated indignation today [March 17th] over the state's hiring of former Republican Gov. Thomas E. Dewey. . . .
> Democrats in the Senate shouted "fraud" and "shame" and shook accusing fingers at the Republicans.
> "It's not only fraud, it's criminal," cried Majority Leader Joseph Zaretzki, "using public money for private purposes for the preservation and protection of the Republican party."
> Time and again during the Senate clash, which raged for nearly an hour, the Democrats asked why the Republican administration had hired Mr. Dewey instead of relying on the State Attorney General, Louis J. Lefkowitz.

On March 25, the three-judge Federal District Court extended the deadline for reapportioning the state legislature from April 1 to May 5, 1965. Commenting on this extension in an editorial entitled, "Democratic Opportunity," the New York *Times* observed:

> Postponement of the deadline for legislative reapportionment of New York State . . . gives the Democrats now in control of the legislature a splendid opportunity to redeem themselves. By producing a fair and equitable plan, free from the gerrymandering that marred the Republican redistricting efforts, the Democrats would go a long way toward erasing from public memory the disgraceful partisan squabble that kept them from the state's urgent business during the early weeks of the session.*

• • •

* Following their victory in the November election, the Democrats assumed control of the legislature; however, a struggle for power between the upstate

There is a clear, obvious need for legislation to fill the void [left by the invalidation by Justice Levy of all four apportionment acts]. The Democratic party has pledged itself to support the creation of an independent bipartisan commission to draw new district lines that would be compact and contiguous and not based on party enrollment. It should go forward speedily to keep this promise before the expiration of the new deadline.

"STATE REDISTRICTING LAW KILLED BY APPEALS COURT" read the headlines of the Thursday, April 15, New York *Times*. The previous day, by a 6-1 vote, New York's highest court had upheld Justice Levy's decision in *In the Matter of Orans*. Speaking for the majority, Chief Judge Charles S. Desmond stated:

We hold to be in full effect the flat, positive and unmistakable command of the state constitution that there be 150 members of the state Assembly. Since each of the four plans violates that command, each plan and all five statutes are invalid.

Judge Francis Bergen, concurring, agreed that the Assembly could not be enlarged beyond 150 members by legislative enactment. "But," he continued, "the limitation of the New York Constitution on legislative power to reapportion districts goes well beyond a mere numerical change in the Assembly districts." It must be remembered, he said, that:

The legislature owes its existence to the constitution. All of its powers, and the limitation on its powers, spring from it. No residual power to make structural changes in its own organization or in other branches of the government set up by the constitution is vested in the legislature. These basic structures may be altered only by the approval of the people.

The fact that the federal government has now declared that the New York Constitution is invalid as in conflict with the United States Constitution in the way it apportions the legislature does not create a

---

Democrats, and proponents and opponents of New York City's Mayor Wagner prevented the selection of Senate and Assembly majority leaders until the Republican leadership joined forces with Wagner's supporters to elect Joseph Zaretzki, and Anthony J. Travia to the two positions respectively.

new kind of ultra-constitutional power to establish a different basic pattern of representation. The people of New York retain the sole power to do this, and it has not been vested by them in the legislature even to meet an emergency created by the federal decisions.

·   ·   ·

To say that New York, one of the states which formed the federal government itself, is to derive a power over the reconstruction of its own government from the intimations of the judicial branch of the federal government as to what powers its legislature, ought to have is both revolutionary doctrine and a constitutional anachronism.

Judge John Van Voorhis, in a sharp dissent, argued that the 150-member provision was an integral part of the apportionment formula which the United States Supreme Court had struck down:

It would be playing fast and loose with the facts to assume that the number of 150 was arrived at independently of the formula in order to fix the numerical membership of the Assembly without regard to how they were to be distributed between upstate and downstate or among the more populous and less populous counties.

By its decision, the Court of Appeals left New York State without a valid plan for apportionment. Referring to this problem, Chief Judge Desmond stated bluntly: "It is up to the legislature now to enact a new districting-apportionment formula." Under the mandate of the Federal District Court, the legislature had precisely twenty-two days—from April 14 to May 5—in which to draft a new act, consistent with the provisions of both the federal and state constitutions.

14

New York Apportionment Acts and the Courts: Part III

The first week of May saw the Democrats desperately trying to prepare and enact a new apportionment plan for New York State in time to meet the May 5 deadline set by the Federal Court. The problems party strategists faced seemed overwhelming. As stated by Sanford E. Stanton in the May 3 edition of the New York *Journal-American:*

> A coalition of Republicans and upstate Democrats is braced to block any redistricting plan to come out of the Democratic-controlled Joint Legislative Commission on Reapportionment.
>
> And even if the plan could leap that hurdle, it still would face a probable veto by Republican Governor Rockefeller, who wants reapportionment under Republican plans drafted by the lame-duck legislature last December.

The political dilemma faced by Democratic leaders failed to evoke any sympathy from R. Peter Straus. In a statement issued May 4, he explained:

> WMCA's interest in the New York State apportionment case is in distributing state legislative seats according to population, in one undiluted vote for every qualified voter in the state. Period.
>
> We hold no more of a brief for a "Partisan Democratic Apportionment" now, in May, than we did for a Republican gerrymander four months ago, in December.

In December, the new majority leaders said that this session would make a straight-forward effort to comply with the Court rulings in our case. They said they would not circumvent those rulings with a partisan "tit for tat."

My party has had four months in office—four months to deliver on its promise of a fair apportionment. Now, in May, we have begun to fret about the fulfillment of that promise.

Our counsel—and disinterested attorneys throughout the state—have made it clear that four months is more than enough time to create a new, fair apportionment.

Yet now, after four months in office, the majority leaders plead insufficient time to meet the Federal Court's deadline this week.

We doubt whether the leadership's eleventh-hour delay means anything more than eleventh-hour rearrangements of district lines to calm bad political nerves.

We question whether the Court will receive better than half-a-loaf —better than a districting for one house only.

And we wonder whether the current frantic effort in Albany will yield more than token compliance with the District Court's order.

We are politically "square": four-square for a special election in November 1965. We believe that full compliance with the District Court's order for such an election is fully possible.

The following day, May 5, the New York *Daily News* reported that radio station WMCA would ask the Federal Court to appoint a special master (a court-appointed referee) to draw up a fair redistricting program in time for use in the November election. Later that day, the Democrats revealed their own districting bill for the Assembly. It shifted fourteen seats from upstate New York to the New York metropolitan region, leaving the former with fifty-six seats and the latter with ninety-four. The Democrats had not had time, however, to draft an apportionment for the Senate.

Five days later, May 10, the Federal District Court, Judges Sterry R. Waterman, Sylvester J. Ryan and Richard H. Levet presiding, conducted a hearing to consider whether the November election should still be held under Plan A which the state Court of Appeals had ruled in violation of the New York State Constitution.

Orrin Judd, representing New York State, insisted that, since the District Court had, on December 1, upheld the validity of Plan A, the November election should take place under that apportionment formula. He denied repeatedly that it would be feasible for the Court to appoint a special master to draft a new apportionment consistent with both the federal and state constitutions.

Leonard Sand accused the legislature of stalling and urged the Court to appoint a special master rather than to force the state to conduct its election under an apportionment formula which had been held to violate the state constitution. He recognized, however, that the Court did have power to order an election under Plan A. He also suggested that weighted-voting could be used on an interim basis.

Although the Judges indicated that they were not necessarily convinced of the efficacy of weighted voting, Sand's proposal did elicit from the Court favorable comment as to his role as an attorney.

> *Judge Ryan:* I want to say, Mr. Sand, that throughout the four years [that the New York apportionment had been litigated in the District Court] you have been of great help to the Court and you have done a wonderful job as a member of the bar of this Court, in my opinion.
>
> *Judge Waterman:* I must say—
>
> *Judge Levet:* Second the motion.
>
> *Judge Waterman:* I must say that the statement you have just made is about as lawyerlike and statesmanlike a statement as you have made in four years.
>
> *Judge Ryan:* Mr. Sand has done a splendid job and so has your associate, Mr. Gross.

After hearing from Nassau County and New York City, both of which supported Sand's position, Judge Waterman announced the opinion of the Court:

> All three of us are of the opinion that there is no point in any further delay with respect to holding an election to elect members of the general Assembly and Senate for the year 1965. Whether there is some purpose in taking away from the duly elected people, duly elected representatives of the people, the right which we wish they would exercise and which we have given them every opportunity to exercise with respect to the legislature which will be elected in 1966 is, of course, another question.

But as of today a majority of the Court is ordering that its previous orders be complied with forthwith, and that Plan A will form the basis for the election of members of the legislature who will hold office for one year, the year 1966, the calendar year, or whenever, and will be elected on November 2, 1965. The machinery of the election process which you gentlemen have told us about so often can therefore begin to operate.

Judge Levet dissented. In his view, the Supreme Court in deciding the Reapportionment Cases intended that only those portions of state constitutions specifically inconsistent with the federal Constitution should be invalidated. Plan A violated legitimate sections of the New York Constitution.

In an editorial entitled "Reapportionment Frolics," the New York *Post* criticized both the Court and the legislature:

The Federal Court's redistricting decision raised highly arguable questions.

As Leonard Sand, attorney for WMCA, pointed out to the Court, there were two forces at work—the GOP, doing everything possible to salvage its own gerrymander in the form of Plan A, and the Democrats, busily striving to avoid an election this fall.

Mr. Sand did not believe the Court had to confine itself to these two dubious options. The dissent of Judge Levet appears to bear him out.

Most citizens will say the Democrats brought this fiasco upon themselves. After Justice Matthew Levy's decision killing Plan A, the Democrats had ample time to turn over the job of redistricting to a non-partisan commission, as they had pledged.

Instead they came up with a gerrymander program even more grotesque than Plan A. At the same time they sought to delay the whole operation in the hope of forcing the Court to cancel the 1965 election.

Understandably this did not set well with the Court. Two of the Court's three judges ruled elections should be held even if they have to be held under Plan A and even though that plan had been ruled invalid by the state's Court of Appeals.

The legislature has until May 24 to come up with a better proposal. That could be done by enacting into statutory form Judge Levet's proposal for a one-shot election in November on the basis of existing district lines, plus the use of weighted voting.

This would be a temporary expedient. If the proposal were combined with the establishment of a non-partisan commission to prepare a plan for the 1966 elections and the calling of a constitutional convention, the package would partially wipe out the dishonorable character of the legislature's performance to date.

On May 18, the Democratic leaders of the legislature announced that they had hired former Federal Judge Simon H. Rifkind to spearhead a movement to evade a special election in November under Plan A. They also stated that they would call for a constitutional convention to revise completely the state's legislative districting laws to make them conform with the one-man, one-vote ruling of the Supreme Court. Moreover, Assembly Speaker Anthony J. Travia pledged that the legislature would immediately enact two bills: One to provide for "weighted" votes for members elected from the present legislative districts; the other to establish a non-legislative, bipartisan commission to study the districting problem and report by December 1, 1965.

The following day, the legislature did, in fact, pass a concurrent resolution.

Declaring the course of action to be taken by the legislature before the recess or adjournment of its 1965 regular session with respect to interim and long-range solutions of the problems attendant upon the reapportionment of the Senate and Assembly districts of the state and memorializing the Governor of the state to approve legislation passed at the present session submitting the questions of holding a constitutional convention to the electorate of the state at the general election in November nineteen hundred, sixty-five.

However, by May 24, when the District Court met again to hand down its formal order, the Democrats had been able to pass neither of their promised apportionment acts. Despite an eloquent appeal by Simon Rifkind on behalf of the delinquent legislature, the Court, Judge Levet dissenting, upheld its May 10 ruling: The November election would take place, as scheduled, under Plan A.

Despite the finality of the Court's holdings, the Democrats did not give up. James Desmond, writing from Albany in the May 24 New York *Daily News,* reported:

> The Democrats in the legislature got together today and doggedly passed their stop-gap reapportionment bills, but the move apparently came too late.
>
> For while the Democrats were debating the bills a three-judge federal court in New York City was ordering a special legislative election for November—the very ruling that the Democratic bills were designed to head off.
>
> The ruling was announced on the floor, but the debate went ahead anyway because the Democrats were trying to establish a record of legislative action as the basis for an appeal to the U.S. Supreme Court from the lower court's ruling.
>
> The bills, passed on party line votes, provide:
>
> For appointment of a bipartisan commission of 12—six to be named by the Governor and three each by the temporary president of the Senate and the Assembly Speaker—to draw up a reapportionment scheme and report back by Dec. 1. . . .
>
> For a system of weighted voting in the 1966 session of the legislature to give legislators elected from the existing districts—which were outlawed last year by the U.S. Supreme Court—voting power proportionate to the number of people they represent.
>
> The bills now go to Governor Rockefeller for his signature, but their fate is in doubt, particularly the weighted voting proposal which was denounced by the New York Federal Court even before the legislature voted on it.

Three days later, May 27, the fate of the Democratic bills was determined: Governor Rockefeller vetoed both. His reasons were that reapportionment was the responsibility of the legislature, not of a so-called neutral body, and that weighted voting was unconstitutional.

Also on May 27, Associate Justice John Marshall Harlan heard arguments on whether the District Court's order should be stayed. Judge Rifkind, representing the Democratic leaders of the New York legislature urged a stay of the lower Court's order on grounds that it would "wreak havoc" with the state's political processes, and force the state and political parties to spend substantial sums preparing for the election. Orrin Judd, representing the office of the New York Attorney General and the New York Secretary of State insisted that the District Court's "unanimous determination and firm resolve that there be an election this year must be respected." At the end of an hour-and-a-half long closed session, Justice Harlan announced that, because of the great importance of the case, he would refer the matter to the entire Supreme Court.

While the Court was deciding whether or not to issue a stay order, a New York *Times* editorial berated Governor Rockefeller for vetoing the two Democratic apportionment bills.

THE GOVERNOR'S VETOES

Governor Rockefeller was wrong to veto the measure passed by the Democratic-controlled legislature for a bipartisan commission to guide the drawing of new legislative district lines. Regardless of the motives that led the Democrats to enact this measure so belatedly, it is regrettable that the Governor did not give greater consideration to the merits of the proposal.

Experience has shown that the only practicable way of eliminating the twin evils of malapportionment and gerrymandering is to take the drawing of new district lines out of the hands of the legislature and put them under control of a body less subject to immediate political pressures.

.   .   .

The commission vetoed by Governor Rockefeller would have been charged with drawing up a redistricting plan by December 1, for submission to the legislature next January. This provision would have amply protected the legislature's right of final decision.

Governor Rockefeller also vetoed a companion bill put through by the Democrats, which would have provided for the use of the present legislative districts, but with weighted voting to overcome population discrepancies. The Governor's comment that this was plainly a violation of both the federal and state constitutions showed very little respect for Federal Judge Richard H. Levet, who originally advanced the suggestion in his dissent from the majority ruling.

On June 1, the Supreme Court, in a brief per curiam opinion, refused to stay the District Court's order with Justice Harlan dissenting
sharply.

R. Peter Straus commented contentedly that "the high court ruling
closes the books on more than seventy years of legalized malapportionment. It means a new legislative election this year. And it will
mean a new balance of fair representation for cities and suburbs
across the state." Republicans were generally jubilant. The Democrats
viewed the decision less enthusiastically.

The New York *Times,* in a June 2 editorial, indicated strong
dissatisfaction with the Court's decision and the performances of both
the Democratic and Republican parties.

> On Nov. 2 New York State voters will elect a new legislature of 65
> Senators and 165 Assemblymen for one-year terms, on the basis of
> flamboyantly gerrymandered district lines provided in the reappor-
> tionment plan put across by the Republicans last December. This is
> the meaning of the United States Supreme Court's refusal yesterday
> to accede to the request of the Democratic leaders to delay the election.
>
> The plight in which the Democratic party now finds itself arouses
> no sympathy. It must contest the election this fall on such unfavor-
> able terms only because of the disgraceful failure of the present,
> Democratic-controlled, legislature to use the opportunity it has had
> since January to enact a more equitable reapportionment statute. It
> is no secret that some Democrats, at least, were gambling on the hope
> that the Court would cancel the election. They lost, as they deserved
> to lose.
>
> But the citizens of New York are now being compelled by the
> federal courts to vote under a reapportionment measure that has
> been held to violate the state's constitution by the highest tribunal of
> the state, the Court of Appeals. It seems to us that this more than
> justifies the angry dissent by Justice John Marshall Harlan, who pro-
> tested the "casual way" in which the Supreme Court refused a hear-
> ing on the application for the stay.
>
> However, the issue of this fall's election has now been finally set-
> tled. The immediate task is for the state to prepare a reapportion-
> ment plan for 1966 and thereafter, valid under both the state and
> federal constitutions. Governor Rockefeller has—most unwisely—
> vetoed the bill for creation of a bipartisan commission to draw up a

districting plan to recommend to the next legislature. Now the latter will have to start all over in January. It can learn a great deal from the mistaken predecessors to use reapportionment for gross partisan advantage. The question is: Will it?

15

The Last Word

The Federal Court had ordered New York State to hold a special election in November, 1965, under an apportionment formula that violated the state constitution. The question, as the New York *Times* stated in a June 2 editorial, was whether the legislature would take the necessary steps to insure that by the election of November, 1966, New York would have an apportionment which met the standards set by both the federal and state constitutions. Indications were that they would.

Senate Majority Leader Joseph Zaretzki announced on June 11 that he would fight for a state-wide referendum in July so there could be a constitutional convention in the spring for the purpose of drawing new district lines. Four days later, Governor Rockefeller signed the Democratic bill into law.

The orderly manner in which the legislature had proceeded to provide for a new apportionment act contrasted sharply with the obstructionist antics of a few desperate Democratic politicians and of the judges of New York's courts. On June 21, 1965, Professor Robert B. Fleming of the University of Buffalo Law School, representing State Senator Frank J. Glinski, instituted action in the New York State Supreme Court in Albany demanding that there be no election in 1965 and that legislators remain in office until December 31, 1966. The following day, Justice John H. Pennock signed an order to show cause why the desired relief should not be granted. A hearing was set for June 28.

On June 29, a United Press International bulletin reported that Justice Russell Hunt of the State Supreme Court, after hearing oral arguments on Glinski's motion to prevent the special election, reserved decision despite the fact that all parties to the suit urged speedy disposition of the case, noting that June 29 was the first day for circulating nominating petitions for legislative office. The following Friday, July 5, Justice Hunt handed down his decision: He issued an order enjoining the secretary of state from conducting an election under Plan A.

The Appellate Division of the Supreme Court, announcing in a per curiam opinion that "we consider that we are bound, and that our decision must be controlled, by the order of the three-judge District Court [mandating a November, 1965 election]," summarily reversed the lower state court's decision. The stage was thus set for an appeal to New York's highest court, the Court of Appeals.

"STATE'S HIGHEST COURT, 4-3, BARS ELECTING A LEGISLATURE IN FALL AS FEDERAL COURT HAD ORDERED" blared the headline of the July 10 New York *Times*. Chief Judge Charles S. Desmond wrote the majority opinion and was joined by Associate Judges Marvin R. Dye and John F. Scileppi. Associate Judge Adrian Burke wrote a concurring opinion. A dissenting memorandum was filed by Associate Judges Stanley H. Field, John Van Voorhis, and Francis Bergan. Judge Bergan also wrote a separate dissent.

In his opinion for the Court, Chief Judge Desmond, stating that he had seen "no binding federal court order forbidding [the state courts] to deal with this problem of state government," asserted that "neither federal supremacy nor the rules against interference with federal courts by state courts have any application here." The state constitution was explicit: Elections were to be held every other year and the Assembly was to number 150. Plan A violated both of these prescriptions.

"Basically," Desmond reasoned, "the question is: Shall we obey the positive directions of our own state constitution in the absence of a controlling decision elsewhere commanding that an unconstitutional election be held? I answer 'Yes.' The injunction prayed for must be granted."

In a brief concurring opinion Judge Burke noted that the time and method of holding an election for state officials is a state question,

that the United States Supreme Court had directed that the greatest
possible deference should be paid to state action and that the high
court "had directed that an election be held in 1965 only if there is
a valid legislative apportionment." Plan A was invalid under the
state constitution. "Therefore an election this year," Burke reasoned,
"can only be held constitutionally by providing that the proper number of legislators be elected at large."

In their dissenting memorandum, Judges Bergan, Field, and
Voorhis took sharp issue with the majority as to the question of the
applicability of federal supremacy. Noting that "the decision now
being handed down serves only to further confound a most unfortunate and confused situation," the three dissenting judges asserted:

> For the courts of this state now to grant injunctive relief, prevent-
> ing the holding of an election in 1965, would be in direct conflict
> with the District Court's decision, a decision which, in view of the
> Supreme Court's recent denial of an application for a stay, has that
> tribunal's implicit approval. Such a conflict between federal and state
> judicial power should be avoided in the interest of the public order
> and the proper administration of justice.

Judge Bergen, in a separate dissent, emphasized even more emphatically that the Court of Appeals was, in effect, engaging in a direct
struggle for power with the federal courts:

> . . . [T]o grant a state court injunction against the enforcement of a
> federal court order amounts to a confrontation of power which
> ought to be avoided if possible, in the interest of orderly government
> within the federal union, entirely aside from the vagaries of the
> supremacy clause as applied to a situation of this kind.
>
> The result of the decision now being made is that a court of one
> sovereign authority has directed the New York Secretary of State to
> prepare an election in 1965 and the court of another sovereign au-
> thority has prohibited him from doing just that.
>
> The legal difficulties over the exercise of the power of New York to
> govern itself can be resolved definitely by the Supreme Court of the
> United States in reviewing the decision of this court; and cannot be

resolved adequately by a clash of conflicting orders between the New York Supreme Court and the United States District Court.

Martin Arnold, in a July 10 article in the New York *Times,* reported that "reaction to the State Court of Appeals ruling yesterday barring a special legislative election this fall ranged from delight to distress."

Mayor Wagner was quoted as stating that the decision "certainly eliminates the danger of an atypical, abnormal election," the results of which "would be completely nonrepresentative in a state-wide sense." In contrast, New York City Comptroller Abraham Beame, a candidate for the Democratic nomination for mayor, announced that "while I have great reservations about the Rocky-mandered Plan A, I favor an election this November, and I support any and all attempts to appeal this decision to the Supreme Court, which wisely set down the mandate of one man, one vote."

In another article, written by *Times* reporter Sidney E. Zion, Leonard Sand was said to have referred to the Court of Appeals ruling as "trivia of the highest degree." "We'll ask the Federal Court to have this set aside," Sand allegedly continued. "If the state court doesn't like the form of the Federal Court's original order I'm sure the Federal Court will issue an order that removes any ambiguities. The Federal Court has the last word." (Immediately after publication of Zion's article, Sand, claiming to be misquoted, wrote to assure Judge Desmond that he "would certainly never characterize any decision of the Court of Appeals as being 'trivial.' ")

The New York *Times,* in a July 10 editorial entitled, "Compounding Confusion," sharply criticized Judge Desmond's decision:

> The Court of Appeals, New York State's highest judicial tribunal, ruled yesterday that the special legislative election scheduled in November could not be held because it violated the state constitution in at least two respects. By doing so it placed itself in direct opposition to the United States District Court's order that the election must be held under Republican Plan A.
> Associate Judge Stanley Field did not exaggerate when he wrote in his dissenting opinion that the decision, reached by a 4-to-3 vote, "serves only to confound the most unfortunate and confusing situa-

tion." The minority argued that a conflict between the federal and state courts should be avoided "in the interest of the public order and the proper administration of justice."

．　．　．

To the layman, it would seem clear that under the supremacy clause of Article VI of the United States Constitution the decision of the Federal Court would be binding. But Judge Desmond explicitly stated that in his view the supremacy clause did not apply to the case before him. . . .

Those favoring the fall election will surely go back to the Federal Court and ask it to reaffirm its order. Meanwhile it is possible that the episode will form the basis for another appeal to Justice Harlan of the United States Supreme Court for a stay of the election until the nation's highest tribunal has heard and decided the case, probably long after November. The issue which seemed settled in May is once more wide open.

On July 10, Federal District Judge Sylvester J. Ryan, acting at the request of Attorney General Louis J. Lefkowitz, issued a temporary order enjoining all state proceedings in conflict with the three-judge Federal Court ruling of May 24 calling for the election of a new legislature November 2 under Plan A. A hearing was set for Tuesday, July 13.

Also on July 10, *Times* writer Sidney E. Zion reported that Judge Waterman, in a telephone interview, when asked whether a "final and binding order" had been issued by the District Court, replied "Gee, I don't know. We thought we were binding the litigants." After reading aloud the District Court's order, Waterman reportedly asked, "Are there any words you can think of that would have made that clearer?"

Two days later, the situation became even more confused as Senate Majority Leader Joseph Zaretzki and Assembly Speaker Anthony J Travia sent a telegram to Justice John Marshall Harlan of the United States Supreme Court requesting that he stay the Federal Court order directing that the November election be held.

Operating under threat of a Supreme Court injunction, Judges Levet, Ryan, and Waterman began their hearing July 13 on the question of whether they should enjoin all interference with the conducting of the November election.

Orrin Judd, representing New York State, assured the District Court that "if there is chaos now, I think it is not this Court's fault; but I think the Court, having issued the order of May 24, has the power to create order instead of chaos." As evidence of the power of the District Court, Judd quoted from an opinion in the Little Rock School Case,* *Brown* v. *Board of Education,* wherein the Court of Appeals for the Eighth Circuit said:

> We have no doubt whatever that the Federal District Court . . . had the power and the duty . . . in order to protect or effectuate its judgments, to stay the state court proceedings. A federal court should not, when prompt action is required, be compelled to indulge in useless formalities in protecting its judgments from being emasculated by state court proceedings.

Leonard Sand, after pointing out the repeated failure of the legislature, under both Republican and Democratic control, to enact an apportionment valid under both the state and federal constitutions, noted that "if there is today no ready accommodations between the provisions of the Fourteenth Amendment and the provisions of the state constitution, the responsibility for that unfortunate situation lies outside this courtroom." Sand argued that: "The basic problem in the whole area of apportionment has been the failure to recognize that we are dealing with a personal civil right guaranteed by the Fourteenth Amendment. If this were a voting case in a racial context, and if we were in some other state, there would be no hesitation at all in recognizing that federal supremacy is absolutely essential if the rights guaranteed by the Constitution are to be meaningful."

Judge Simon K. Rifkind, representing Senator Zaretzki and Assemblyman Travia, after conceding that the District Court had the power to override the state court and force a November election, argued that:

---

* Following a Federal District Court order that Little Rock's Central High School be desegregated, a citizen of the city obtained an Arkansas state court order enjoining the school board from opening the schools.

The issue this morning before your Honors is not whether this Court has the power and the determination to do what it has said it should do, the question is should it in the exercise of its wisdom, in the exercise of its discretion, in the exercise of the high function committed to its care under the Constitution, do what it has proposed to do.

I have come here this morning, may it please the Court, to champion two unpopular notions, or notions that I think are currently unpopular and in disfavor. The first of these is an almost forgotten idea of federalism. The second one is a more universal concept of moderation.

. . . Federalism is a state of mind, it is an attitude, it is a relationship, but in practice federalism means this, that when two sovereigns rule in the same territory and rule over the same people, they must so behave that they do not unnecessarily jostle each other.

The Court was visibly unimpressed by Rifkind's arguments. At the close of the hearing, Judge Waterman, addressing Orrin Judd, said, "You must have some hope at least of winning your point. Do you have a prepared order?" Utilizing Judd's offered order, the Court, following a recess of less than fifteen minutes, returned to deliver its opinion.

Judge Waterman, caustically referring to Judge Desmond's statement that he had seen no "final and binding order," stated:

We intended the order of this Court of May 24, 1965, to be exactly such an order, so directing. We believe the order did expressly state such a judgment, but to remove any question as to its purpose, intent or wording, we are entering a further order containing mandatory and injunctive provisions.

Speaking for a unanimous court (including Judge Levet who reluctantly indicated that despite his earlier opposition, he would concur because "a shift [in the status of the election] would create endless confusion"), Judge Waterman ordered that:

Frank J. Glinski, William F. Keenan, and all parties to this action, their agents, attorneys and servants, their successors and all other persons are hereby forever restrained and enjoined from interfering with the carrying out and execution by any and all New York State officers and election officials and their successors and all other persons of the order of this court of May 24, 1965 [requiring a November, 1965 election under Reapportionment Plan A].

The decision of the District Court was greeted by an almost universal sigh of relief. The election would take place, and a direct clash between the federal and state courts seemed to have been averted. The New York *Times,* however, mirrored the opinion of many when it expressed regret that the election would take place "under a highly partisan and unconstitutional" apportionment plan:

> The Federal Court was quite right in not letting the Democrats get away with their obvious efforts to block the election entirely. There should be an election in November. On that point Judge Richard J. Levet, who dissented from the designation of Plan A by the majority of the Court, was in agreement with the others. He pointed out yesterday that the preparation of the election machinery was already in progress and that any change now would only cause further confusion.
>
> But how much better off the State of New York might be today if the Court had granted the motion of counsel for radio station WMCA . . . and appointed a special master last March to prepare a nonpartisan apportionment plan for use in the event the legislature failed to act. The Court indicated yesterday its intention to follow this procedure next year if necessary but meanwhile it will have imposed an unconstitutional legislature on the state.

The Democrats, however, refused to give up their fight to block the fall election. On July 14, they filed a new petition with United States Supreme Court Justice John M. Harlan seeking a stay of the latest District Court order. Their attempt proved futile. On Friday, July 17, Justice Harlan refused to bar the November election.

In a brief memorandum opinion, Harlan said:

> Were [the United States Supreme Court] in session I would have referred both of these applications [for stays] to it for disposition, as was done with the earlier application for a stay of the District Court's order of May 24. I consider it, however, my duty in the circumstances

to act on these applications myself, deeming that I would not be justified in asking the Chief Justice to take steps to convene the Court in special session. Given what has already transpired, I am left in no doubt as to what the decision on these applications must be.

While I have heretofore expressed my strong disagreement both with this Court's basic state reapportionment decisions and with the Court's subsequent refusal, at least so far, to give plenary considera- tion to any of the challenges that have been made to the particular kinds of relief granted by district courts, nevertheless I can only conclude that the denial of these applications is compelled by this Court's earlier summary denial of a stay pending appeal of the District Court's order of May 24 directing the election in question. That denial surely signified this Court's unwillingness to interfere with the District Court's direction of the election, even though the election was to be held under a plan of apportionment which violated the New York Constitution. That being so, the supremacy clause of the federal Constitution requires the state courts to give recognition to the District Court's order.

·   ·   ·

In conclusion, I think it pertinent to observe that these applications illustrate how important it is for this Court to act in a sensitive and not heavy-handed manner in this novel and delicate constitutional field. It is manifest from the majority opinion of the New York Court of Appeals that this present unfortunate situation would not have arisen had [the Supreme Court] explicated its reasons for refusing to stay the District Court's order of May 24.

In New York, Mayor Wagner expressed the opinion of most New Yorkers when he commented: "The last word has now been said. The problems held in abeyance pending this final action must now be confronted." Whether the legislature and the Courts would be able to come to an agreement over a valid reapportionment of New York State remained an open question. Reapportionment will continue to be an important issue in New York politics and an issue that per- haps may never be completely resolved satisfactorily either in the courts or the political arena.

Conclusion

The legislative and legal skirmishes that have taken place in New York State have been colorful and at times, heated. Yet they have occurred within the framework of a fundamental recognition by all participants that the Supreme Court's decision in *WMCA* v. *Lomenzo* was final and authoritative and must, in a reasonable amount of time, be implemented. Experiences in other states point in the same direction: Reapportionment, unlike school desegregation, will proceed with "all deliberate speed."

What is less certain, however, is what in fact constitutes compliance with the Court's one man, one vote mandate. The Supreme Court, it will be recalled, did not enunciate specific constitutional standards. The Chief Justice called for "substantial equality," not "mathematical exactness." There appear to be two major alternatives: The Court, on the one hand, can set definite limits on the deviations from absolute equality—perhaps, districts could vary up to 10 per cent above or below a state-wide average—or, on the other hand, the Court could judge each apportionment separately, on the basis of the specific conditions existing in each state. If the Court chooses the latter alternative, the problem of whether a state's apportionment is fair will have to be reconsidered following each reapportionment.

A second problem that the Supreme Court will eventually have to face is how far the one man, one vote decision should be extended. Already there have been conflicting decisions in state and federal courts as to whether counties, cities, and other political subdivisions must also meet the equal population standard.

The Supreme Court here, as in the entire area of individual rights, has filled a void left by the inaction of the political branches of the government. In so doing it has returned to the people the essence of representative democracy—the right of the individual to have his vote count equally.

Source Notes

Most of the material for this book was drawn directly from court decisions, court transcripts, newspaper articles, briefs, materials from the files of the litigants and personal interviews. The following source notes include cases and articles cited in the chapters as well as helpful reference materials.

Chapter 1: WMCA Decides to Litigate

Baker v. *Carr,* 369 U.S. 186 (1962).
Colegrove v. *Green,* 328 U.S. 549 (1946).
Dyer v. *Kazuhisa Abe,* 138 F. Supp. 220 (D. Hawaii 1956), *rev'd. as moot,* 256 F. 2d 729 (9th Cir. 1958).
Gomillion v. *Lightfoot,* 364 U.S. 339 (1960).
Magraw v. *Donovan,* 159 F. Supp. 901 (D. Minn. 1958), *juris. retained,* 163 F. Supp. 184 (D. Minn. 1958), *dismissed on plaintiff's motion,* 177 F. Supp. 803 (D. Minn. 1959).

POLITICAL QUESTIONS

Bickel, Alexander M., "The Durability of *Colegrove* v. *Green,* 72 *Yale Law Journal* 39 (1962).
Emerson, Thomas I., "Malapportionment and Judicial Power," 72 *Yale Law Journal* 64 (1962).
McKay, Robert B., *Reapportionment.* New York: Twentieth Century Fund, 1965.

JUDICIAL RESTRAINT VS. JUDICIAL ACTIVISM

Bickel, Alexander M., *The Least Dangerous Branch: The Supreme Court at the Bar of Politics.* Indianapolis: Bobbs-Merrill, 1962.

Black, Charles L., *The People and the Court.* New York: The Macmillan Company, 1960.

Frankfurter, Felix, "Self-Willed Judges and the Judicial Function," reprinted in Alan F. Westin, ed., *An Autobiography of the Supreme Court.* New York: The Macmillan Company, 1963.

Freund, Paul A., *The Supreme Court of the United States.* Cleveland: Meridian Books, 1961.

Gunther, Gerald, "The Subtle Vices of the 'Passive Virtues'—A Comment on Principles and Expediency in Judicial Review," 64 *Columbia Law Review* 1 (1964).

Hand, Learned, *The Bill of Rights.* Cambridge: Harvard University Press, 1958.

Jackson, Robert H., *The Supreme Court in the American System of Government.* Cambridge: Harvard University Press, 1955.

Wechsler, Herbert, "Toward Neutral Principles of Constitutional Law," 73 *Harvard Law Review* 1 (1959).

GROWTH OF THE FOURTEENTH AMENDMENT

Mason, Alpheus J., *The Supreme Court from Taft to Warren.* Baton Rouge: Louisiana State University Press, 1958.

McCloskey, Robert G., *The American Supreme Court.* Chicago: University of Chicago Press, 1960.

McKay, Robert B., *Reapportionment.* New York: Twentieth Century Fund, 1965.

Pritchett, C. Herman, *The Roosevelt Court: A Study in Judicial Politics and Values, 1937-1947.* New York: Octagon Books, 1963.

LAW REVIEW RESPONSE TO *Colegrove*

Lewis, Anthony, "Legislative Apportionment and the Federal Courts," 71 *Harvard Law Review* 1057 (1958).

Note, "Constitutional Right to Congressional Districts of Equal Population," 56 *Yale Law Journal* 127 (1946).

Note, "Reapportionment of Congressional Districts in Illinois," 41 *Illinois Law Review* 578 (1946).

Chapter 2: A Case is Begun

Gomillion v. *Lightfoot,* 364 U.S. 339 (1960).
MacDougall v. *Green,* 335 U.S. 281 (1948).
WMCA v. *Simon,* 196 F. Supp. 758 (S.D.N.Y. 1961), 202 F. Supp. 741 (S.D.N.Y. 1962); 208 F. Supp. 368 (S.D.N.Y. 1962).
See also: *Cook* v. *Fortson,* 329 U.S. 675 (1946); *South* v. *Peters,* 339 U.S. 276 (1950); and *Wright* v. *Rockefeller,* 376 U.S. 52, 84 S. Ct. 603 (1964) *affirming* 211 F. Supp. 460 (S.D.N.Y. 1962).

Comment, "Federal Constitutional Limitation on State Power Over Political Subversion," 61 *Columbia Law Review* 704 (1961).
Note, "Judicial Attitude Toward Political Question Doctrine: The Gerrymander and Civil Rights," 1960 *Washington University Law Quarterly* 292 (1960).
Note, "*Wright* v. *Rockefeller* and Legislative Gerrymanders: The Desegregation Decisions Plus a Problem of Proof," 72 *Yale Law Journal* 1041 (1963).

Chapter 3: Baker v. *Carr:* A Judicial Landmark

Baker v. *Carr,* 369 U.S. 186 (1962).

Black, Charles L., "Inequities in Districting for Congress: *Baker* v. *Carr* and *Colegrove* v. *Green,*" 72 *Yale Law Journal* 13 (1962).
Dixon, Robert, "Legislative Apportionment and the Federal Constitution," 27 *Law and Contemporary Problems* 329 (1962).
Emerson, Thomas I., "Malapportionment and Judicial Power," 72 *Yale Law Journal* 64 (1962).
Friedelbaum, Stanley H., "*Baker* v. *Carr:* The New Doctrine of Judicial Intervention and Its Implications for American Federalism," 29 *University of Chicago Law Review* 673 (1962).
Israel, Jerold, "On Charting a Course Through the Mathematical Quagmire: The Future of *Baker* v. *Carr,*" 61 *Michigan Law Review* 107 (1962).
Lancaster, Robert, "What's Wrong with *Baker* v. *Carr,*" 15 *Vanderbilt Law Review* 1247 (1962).
McCloskey, Robert G., "Foreword: The Reapportionment Case," 76 *Harvard Law Review* 54 (1962).
McKay, Robert B., "Political Thickets and Crazy Quilts: Reapportionment and Equal Protection," 61 *Michigan Law Review* 645 (1963).

Chapter 4: Politics of Apportionment

WMCA v. *Simon,* 370 U.S. 190 (1962).

Baker, Gordon E., *Rural vs. Urban Political Power.* New York: Random House, 1963.

Harvard, William C. and Loren P. Beth, *The Politics of Misrepresentation.* Baton Rouge: Louisiana State University Press, 1962.

Silva, Ruth C., *Legislative Apportionment,* 2 vols. Staff Report No. 33. New York: State of New York Temporary Commission on Revision and Simplification of the Constitution, April, 1960.

————, "Apportionment of the New York Assembly," 31 *Fordham Law Review* 1 (1962).

————, "Apportionment of the New York Legislature," 55 *American Political Science Review* 870 (1961).

————, "Apportionment of the New York Senate," 30 *Fordham Law Review* 595 (1962).

————, "Legislative Representation—With Special Reference to New York," 27 *Law and Contemporary Problems* 408 (1962).

————, "The Population Base for Apportionment of the New York Legislature," 32 *Fordham Law Review* 1 (1963).

Tyler, Gus and David I. Wells, "New York: Constitutionally Republican," in Malcolm E. Jewell, ed., *The Politics of Reapportionment.* New York: Atherton Press, 1962.

Chapter 5: A Trial on the Merits

Baker v. *Carr,* 369 U.S. 186 (1962).
WMCA v. *Simon,* 208 F. Supp. 368 S.D.N.Y. (1962).

United States Advisory Commission on Intergovernmental Relations, *Apportionment of State Legislatures.* Washington, 1962.

Chapter 6: Before the High Court

DeGrazia, Alfred, *Essay on Apportionment and Representative Government.* Washington: American Enterprise Institute for Public Policy Research, 1963.

McKay, Robert B., *Reapportionment and the Federal Analogy.* New York: National Municipal League, 1962.

Chapter 7: How the Supreme Court Decides

Clark, Tom C., "The Supreme Court Conference," 19 *Federal Rules Decisions* 303 (1956).

Frankfurter, Felix, "The Supreme Court in the Mirror of Justices," 105 *University of Pennsylvania Law Review* 781 (1957).

Harlan, John Marshall, "What Part Does the Oral Agreement Play in the Conduct of an Appeal," 41 *Cornell Law Review* 6 (1955).

Schmidhauser, John R., *The Supreme Court: Its Politics, Personalities and Procedures*. New York: Holt, Rinehart & Winston, 1960.

Schubert, Glendon, *Judicial Decision-Making*. New York: Free Press, 1963.

Chapter 8: One Man, One Vote

Davis v. *Mann*, 377 U.S. 678 (1964).

Lucas v. *Colorado General Assembly*, 377 U.S. 713 (1964).

Maryland Committee v. *Tawes*, 377 U.S. 656 (1964).

Reynolds v. *Sims*, 377 U.S. 533 (1964).

Roman v. *Sincock*, 377 U.S. 695 (1964).

Wesberry v. *Sanders*, 376 U.S. 1 (1964).

WMCA v. *Lomenzo*, 377 U.S. 633 (1964).

Auerbach, Carl, "The Reapportionment Cases: One Person, One Vote— One Vote, One Value," 1964 *Supreme Court Review* 1.

Kauper, Paul G., "Some Comments on the Reapportionment Cases," 63 *Michigan Law Review* 243 (1964).

Note, "Beyond *Wesberry:* State Apportionment and Equal Protection," 39 *New York University Law Review* 264 (1964).

Note, "*Wesberry* v. *Sanders:* Deep in the Thicket," 32 *George Washington Law Review* 1076 (1964).

Weiss, Jonathan, "Analysis of *Wesberry* v. *Sanders*," 38 *Southern California Law Review* 67 (1965).

Chapter 9: Congress vs. the Court

Black, Charles L., Jr., "The Proposed Amendment of Article V: A Threatened Disaster," 72 *Yale Law Journal* 957 (1963).

Dixon, Robert G., "Reapportionment in the Supreme Court and Congress," 63 *Michigan Law Review* 209 (1964).

Dixon, Robert G., "The Reapportionment Amendments and Direct Democracy," 36 *State Government* 117 (1965).

McKay, Robert B., "Court, Congress and Reapportionment," 63 *Michigan Law Review* 255 (1964).

———, "Don't Amend the Constitution," 38 *State Government* 121 (1965).

Note, "Limitations on the Appellate Jurisdiction of the Supreme Court," 20 *University of Pittsburgh Law Review* 99 (1958).

Chapter 10: Back to the District Court

Baldwin, Fletcher N., Jr. and Stanley K. Laughlin, Jr., "The Reapportionment Cases: A Study in the Constitutional Adjudication Process," 17 *University of Florida Law Review* 301 (1964).

Israel, Jerold, "Nonpopulation Factors Relevant to an Acceptable Standard of Apportionment," 38 *Notre Dame Lawyer* 499 (1963).

Jewell, Malcolm, "Minority Representation: A Political or Judicial Question," 53 *Kentucky Law Journal* 267 (1964-65).

Scanlan, Alfred L., "Problems of Pleading, Proof and Persuasion in a Reapportionment Case," 38 *Notre Dame Lawyer* 415 (1963).

Chapter 11: New York Reapportions Its Legislature

Citizens' Committee on Reapportionment, "Report to Governor Rockefeller," 1964.

Schattschneider, E. E., "Urbanization and Reapportionment," 72 *Yale Law Journal* 7 (1962).

Shull, Charles W., "Political and Partisan Implications of State Legislative Apportionment," 17 *Law and Contemporary Problems* 417 (1952).

Chapter 12: New York Apportionment Acts and the Courts,
              Part I

Banzhaf, John F., "Multi-Member Electoral Districts—Do They Violate the 'One Man, One Vote' Principle?" 76 *Yale Law Journal* 1309 (1966).

Banzhaf, John F., "Weighted Voting Doesn't Work: A Mathematical Analysis," 19 *Rutgers Law Review* 317 (1965).

Engle, Robert H., "Weighting Legislators' Votes to Equalize Representation," 12 *Western Political Quarterly* 422 (1959).

Nagel, Stuart S., "Simplified Bipartisan Computer Redistricting," 17 *Stanford Law Review* 863 (1965).

Roeck, Ernest C., Jr., "Measuring Compactness as a Requirement of Legislative Apportionment," 5 *Midwest Journal of Political Science* 70 (1961).

Weaver, James B. and W. A. Sidney Hess, "A Procedure for Nonpartisan Districting: Development of Computer Techniques," 73 *Yale Law Journal* 289 (1963).

————, "Districting by Machine," 53 *National Civil Review* 293 (1964).

Chapter 13: New York Apportionment Acts and the Courts, Part II

In the Matter of Orans, 15 N.Y. 2d 339, 258 N.Y.S. 2d 825, 206 N.E. 2d 854 (1965).

Bonfield, Arthur Earl, "*Baker* v. *Carr:* New Light on the Constitutional Guarantee of Republican Government," 50 *California Law Review* 245 (1962).

————, "The Guarantee Clause of Article IV, Section 4: A Study in Constitutional Desuetude," 46 *Minnesota Law Review* 513 (1962).

Caruso, Lawrence R., "The Proper Role of the Federal Courts in the Reapportionment of State Legislatures," 36 *Mississippi Law Journal* 300 (1965).

Chapter 14: New York Apportionment Acts and the Courts, Part III

Travia v. *Lomenzo,* 381 U.S. 431 (1965).

Tyler, Gus, "Court versus Legislature," 27 *Law and Contemporary Problems* 390 (1962).

Velvel, Lawrence R., "Suggested Approaches to Constitutional Adjudication and Apportionment," 12 *U.C.L.A. Law Review* 1381 (1965).

Chapter 15: The Last Word

Glinski v. *Lomenzo,* 16 N.Y. 2d 27, 261 N.Y.S. 2d 281, 209 N.E. 2d
277 (1965).